How To Afford Everything

Written By
Dr. Darla Bishop

PRESTIGE
Publishing & Mass Media Company

Dr. Darla Bishop

Contents

HEY YOU,

Let's jump into the world of personal finance together. Finances can have you "*skressed,*" but I promise it doesn't have to be hard, depressing, or sad. Money is fun when you know what do with it. I'm here to teach you the ins and outs of stacking your dollars and getting what you want out of your life.

From navigating budgets to making it rain with investments, we'll laugh, learn, and conquer the money game. Let's face it, being able to manage your 'moolah' is the key to having the ability to do what you want, when you want, wake and plan a vacay to Bali... And who doesn't want that?

"You must gain control over your money,
or the lack of it will forever control you."

-Dave Ramsey

Hello there! I'm Dr. Darla Bishop, and I'm thrilled to introduce my latest book, "How to Afford Everything." This book is deeply meaningful to me, encompassing not only my professional expertise but also my personal voyage towards financial wellness.

Coming from Detroit, I encountered challenges that inspired me to study public health policy and become a financial wellness coach. My fascination with understanding money deepened during my time as a student at the University of Michigan, where I witnessed significant variations in financial lifestyles, sparking a realization of the transformative power of financial knowledge. These experiences have shaped the practical and accessible approach I share in "How to Afford Everything," a step-by-step guide with achievable exercises designed to transform your relationship with money so that you achieve financial wellness.

Having devoured over 100 books on personal finance and self-development, I've distilled my knowledge into this comprehensive guide, sparing you from reading as many. My hope is that this book motivates you to overcome limiting beliefs about wealth, fosters a positive financial mindset, and helps you take the steps needed to Afford Everything. With a touch of wit and relatable anecdotes, I strive to make financial literacy accessible for audiences of all ages and backgrounds. Let's explore together how you can take control of your financial health for a better, more secure future. I'm here to empower you with the lessons that have dramatically changed my life, believing they can do the same for you. I'm excited to be part of your transformative journey.

Dr. Darla Bishop

"If you don't get serious about your money, you won't have serious money"

- Grant Cardone

Chapter One
Real Money Talk

Do you know what it really costs to live the life you want? It's more than just paying the bills; it's about having fun and securing your future. This chapter is all about unmasking your spending habits and getting clear on your financial values. I will also touch on discovering your "magic number," that mystical yet attainable figure that defines your financial goals and dreams. Without it, you are missing a vital piece of the puzzle to affording everything.

Introducing Meka, a determined single mother in her thirties, juggling the responsibilities of parenthood, work, and finances. She often felt like her money was slipping through her fingers, leaving her bank account in a constant state of depletion. Meka's story was not one of financial struggle but rather of financial mystery. Something wasn't adding up, and she couldn't pinpoint where her hard-earned money was going. One day, she decided to work closely with a financial coach (That's me). The first step in our journey together was to gain clarity on her spending habits. Meka revealed that she had developed a routine of withdrawing $200 in cash every time she visited the ATM, and this habit was repeated two to three times a week. It was a significant amount of cash that she was carrying around, and she couldn't track where it was flowing.

To address this, we implemented a "cash diet." Meka agreed to limit her use of cash unless it was for planned expenses. We decided that she could keep $20 in cash on hand for any unexpected school-related expenses her child might have, like a bake sale or field trip. Over the course of forty-five days, we began to unravel the mystery of her disappearing funds. We discovered that a portion of her money was going to good causes, such as supporting small businesses and providing financial assistance to her parents— both admirable endeavors.

However, there was also a significant chunk of money being spent on untrackable expenses. Meka expressed her genuine desire to contribute financially to her parents, who had always been a pillar of support in her life. We devised a plan to make this contribution more structured. She decided on a monthly budget of at least $200 to allocate to her parents. However, she knew her parents might not readily accept her money. To address this, we crafted a script for Meka to approach her mom.

She approached her mom with a proposal. Meka shared that she had been working with a financial coach to gain better control over her money. She expressed her gratitude for her parents' support and her desire to give back. Meka asked if she could take over one of her parents' monthly bills, explaining that it was essential for her to include it in her budget. Her mom, though initially hesitant, agreed to let Meka cover the power bill, which could fluctuate, especially during the winter months. Meka graciously accepted the responsibility, excited to contribute to her parents' well-being. With the implementation of the cash diet, Meka now had a clear understanding of where her money was going.

She could manage her day-to-day expenses more efficiently and allocate funds for upcoming payments or savings towards a vacation. When I checked in with Meka a year after our coaching sessions concluded, she shared her remarkable progress. She had managed to save the equivalent of three months' worth of her salary, a significant financial achievement. This newfound financial security gave her the confidence to pursue a career change she had been postponing for years. The financial cushion provided by her savings allowed her to take the leap, showing her that understanding what it truly cost her to live her best life had opened doors to exciting opportunities and a brighter financial future.

Magic Number

When you want to afford everything, your "**magic number**" is not a mystical incantation or a secret code, but it's certainly as powerful as any spell. Your magic number helps you work toward your goals with confidence and clarity.

Your magic number is the amount of money you need to cover all your expenses, indulge in some fun, and still have some left over to put away for the future. You can calculate it as a monthly number or an annual number. The magic number is that financial equilibrium that ensures your life is comfortably afloat, rather than sinking under the weight of bills and debt. Think of it as a place where you can thrive without financial stress. To calculate your magic number, you'll need to:

1 Determine Your Expenses

Start by tracking your current expenses. This includes fixed costs like rent or mortgage, utilities, groceries, and insurance, as well as discretionary spending on entertainment, dining out, and leisure activities.

2 Set Financial Goals

Consider your short-term and long-term financial goals. Whether it's building an emergency fund, buying a home, or retiring early, your magic number should include provisions for these objectives.

3 Calculate Your Total

Add up your essential expenses, fun and leisure spending, savings and investments, emergency funds, and financial goals. This total is your magic number.

Once you've calculated your magic number, double-check that you put everything in it. Not what you're working with now, not how much you want it to cost you to live, but ***real*** numbers. When you're making a budget, much like planning a party, plan for champagne, spend on sparkling cider, and pad the expenses.

If you are recovering from poverty like I am, this part might be hard. You might have some money habits that helped you survive poverty, maybe you cycle through feast and famine spending. Maybe you are tired of being and feeling poor so you treat yourself. In my own journey, I learned that in order to truly move on and heal from poverty, something I'm still doing, I had to address the past, present, and future at the same time.

Past - You need to have a plan for your debts, family obligations, and past decisions that may be causing problems with your money now. This is not about beating yourself up, because I bet you made those decisions out of survival or based on what you knew then. This is about addressing the consequences of your past decisions without judgment.

Present- It is critically important that you build some comfort and enjoyment into your current life. This is what will help your body reduce its cortisol (stress hormone) load that comes from a tough financial situation. In doing this, you help your brain more easily develop new money habits because you are not in a constant state of deprivation and your body will begin to feel and trust that poverty is truly behind you, or will be soon.

Future- Building your emergency fund and adding in a plan now for the things you want to do, and have, later helps you afford them without acquiring new debts when something unexpected comes up.

Remember, your magic number is not set in stone. The number will change as your life circumstances change. The key is to regularly revisit your financial plan, recalculate your magic number, and adjust your goals and budget accordingly.

Your magic number is more than just a number; it's a ticket to financial freedom. It's your guide to a life where you can confidently pursue your dreams, knowing that you're financially secure. Keep reading for an example of how I calculated my magic number in 2008, right after I graduated from college.

"Money is fun when you have some."
-Darla Bishop

Darla's 2008 Magic Number

Expense	Allotted Funds
$720	Rent
$325	Car Note
$20	Rental Insurance
$100	Phone Bill
$150	Gas
$227	Car Insurance
$40	Utilities
$200	Groceries
$250	Restaurants
$50	Gifts & Parties
$125	Travel Fund
$400	Savings
$100	Family
$1200	Debt
$180	No Roommate

Magic Number=$4137 (Take Home)

Your Money Mindset

Our life experiences, from the earliest days of childhood to the present, significantly influence our beliefs and behaviors about money. The financial values instilled in us during our formative years often linger, affecting the way we manage, spend, save, and invest our money as adults. Understanding this influence is crucial for taking control of your financial future.

Reflect on your childhood and how money was perceived in your family. Was it a source of stability, consistently managed and discussed openly? Or was it marked by financial ups and downs, creating instability and uncertainty? For some, money might have been scarce, making it nearly nonexistent in day-to-day life. These early impressions leave a lasting mark on your financial mindset.

By answering these questions, you'll gain deeper insights into the roots of your money mindset. Understanding how your past experiences influence your financial beliefs and behaviors empowers you to make conscious choices about your financial future. It's the first step towards aligning your financial practices with your goals and values.

- **How did the adults in your life talk about money?**

Communication about money within your family or social circle can reveal a lot about your money mindset. Did the adults in your life openly discuss financial matters, or was money a taboo topic? The way money was talked about or avoided can significantly impact your comfort level with financial conversations.

- When did you open your first bank account(s)?

The act of opening your first bank account can be a significant financial milestone. It often marks the beginning of financial independence and responsibility. Recall the circumstances surrounding this event and how it shaped your perception of saving and managing money.

- What was your first experience investing?

Investing can be both exciting and intimidating. Reflect on your first foray into the world of investments, whether it was purchasing stocks, bonds, or any other financial instruments. How did this experience influence your views on risk and reward in the world of finance?

- Did the adults in your life give you rules about money?

The guidance we receive from adults in our lives, whether parents, teachers, or mentors, can profoundly impact our financial outlook. Were you given specific rules or principles to follow regarding money? Maybe you had to save a portion of your allowance or were only allowed to spend a portion of the monetary gifts you got on your birthday.

- Did you break or change those rules as you got older?

As you grew older and gained more financial independence, you may have questioned or modified the rules imposed by adults in your life. Consider how your financial values evolved and if you adopted new practices that are better aligned with your circumstances and goals.

- What was your first paying job or business? What did you do with the money you earned?

Your initial experiences with earning money, whether through a part-time job, entrepreneurial venture, or chores, can shape your approach to work and income. Reflect on your first earning endeavor and how you utilized the money you earned. Did you spend it freely, save diligently, or something in between?

Splurge vs. Save

A guide to smart spending

The urge to splurge is a siren's song many of us have encountered, a moment of instant gratification that can be as thrilling as it is financially perilous. It's a classic dilemma – the battle between the joy of indulgence and the prudence of saving for the future. Let's unravel the intricate dance of splurge versus save, equipping you with the wisdom to make astute spending decisions that align with your financial aspirations. Before we delve into the strategies for smart spending, let's acknowledge the allure of splurging. The euphoria of acquiring something new, the thrill of dining at your favorite restaurant, or the excitement of a spontaneous treat yo' self day, these moments are enchanting. It's easy to fall into the splurge trap, rationalizing that these indulgences are rewards for your hard work, treats for yourself and that you'll catch up on saving later. Achieving a harmonious balance between splurging and saving feels like something easier said than done but let's break it down.

Indulging in the occasional extravagance can be invigorating. However, unchecked splurging often leads to a cycle of feast and famine. The initial delight of a splurge can quickly turn to guilt, especially if it derails your budget or sabotages your savings goals. This guilt can spiral into financial anxiety, casting a shadow over your overall financial well-being. Smart spending isn't about unyielding frugality or depriving yourself of life's pleasures. It's about making choices that resonate with your values, align with your financial objectives, and create space for both planned and spontaneous splurges without remorse.

Smart spending begins with introspection. What truly matters to you? Experiences like travel, quality time with loved ones, or personal growth? Or perhaps you find joy in possessing the latest gadgets, wearing designer clothes, or driving a newer car?

Your spending should mirror your values. If experiences hold significance, allocate a portion of your budget for travel or memorable outings with friends. If financial security ranks high, focus on eliminating debt and saving.

This doesn't mean relinquishing all indulgences but indulging with purpose. Craft a dedicated splurge budget as part of your comprehensive financial plan. This budget allows you to relish occasional treats without undermining your savings objectives. Knowing you have room for splurges transforms them from guilty pleasures to just part of your budget and a comfortable life.

Before making substantial purchases, investigate different options, compare prices, find coupons and discounts and dig deeper into product reviews. This not only ensures that you receive the best value for your expenditure but also deters impulsive buying. Now, before indulging in a splurge, ensure that your savings goals are met. Commit to saving a portion of your income before designating funds for discretionary spending. This discipline safeguards your financial future.

When you review your spending in chapter 2, pay attention to your past splurges, and assess how the purchase made you feel. Did it genuinely bring happiness and value to your life, or was it a fleeting thrill? Through this reflection, you can refine your spending habits, ensuring they align more closely with your values and priorities. Remember, the aim is not to eradicate splurges but to savor them in moderation while making deliberate choices that support your financial well-being. Striking a balance between splurging and saving empowers you to live a gratifying life today while safeguarding your dreams for the future.

Curbing the Impulse Buy Cravings

In a world filled with enticing advertisements and irresistible deals, curbing impulse buying can feel like a Herculean task. However, mastering the art of curbing impulse purchases is not only financially prudent but also empowering. Impulse buying is the act of making unplanned purchases, often driven by emotions rather than rational decision-making. It can happen to anyone, and it's not limited to a specific age group or income bracket. Whether it's that designer handbag you stumble upon in a boutique, the latest tech gadget that promises to revolutionize your life, or those mouth-watering treats at the checkout counter, impulse purchases have a way of sneaking into our lives.

While the momentary rush of an impulse buy can be exhilarating, it often leads to post-purchase regret. That impulse purchase may disrupt your budget, derail your savings goals, and leave you with buyer's remorse. Recognizing the consequences of these purchases is the first step toward curbing impulse buying.

"Money looks better in the bank than in your closet."

-Anonymous

Check this out..

Now, let's dive into practical strategies to help you make deliberate, thoughtful spending decisions.

Before embarking on any shopping trip, whether online or in-person, draft a list of items you genuinely need. Stick to this list and avoid deviating from it.

Establish a budget for discretionary spending, and adhere to it diligently. Knowing your spending boundaries prevents impulsive splurges.

When faced with an urge to make an unplanned purchase, adopt the "24-hour rule." Give yourself a day to reflect. Often, the initial impulse fades, allowing you to make a rational choice.

Avoid Trigger Environments

Identify environments or situations that trigger impulsive buying tendencies. These may include specific stores, online marketplaces, or social events. Minimize exposure to these triggers whenever possible.

Plastic with guardrails

Paying with cash or using a debit card instead of credit can help you feel the weight of your purchases more tangibly. BUT if you set up your habits the right way, and have a card you can pay off each month, paying with a credit card has some benefits. Many credit cards have built in spending trackers so you can see where your money went. If you know your budget (see chapter 1), you can set your personal limit each month so you don't overspend. You may also earn points or miles that help you pay your bill faster or get discounts on travel.

Unsubscribe and Unfollow

Trim your digital life by unsubscribing from promotional emails and unfollowing brands or retailers on social media. Reducing exposure to marketing tactics lessens the temptation.

Focus on Value, Not Price

Shift your perspective from the price tag to the value a product or experience brings to your life. Consider its long-term usefulness and contribution to your well-being. Things to consider: How long will you be able to use the item? Can you resell it after you're done?

Keep a Spending Journal

Maintain a record of your spending, including impulse purchases. Analyze your spending patterns to identify triggers and areas where you can improve.

Visualize Your Goals

When tempted by an impulse purchase, pause and visualize your financial goals. Look for the money mantra in chapter 1. These goals act as powerful motivators to resist impulsive spending.

By implementing these strategies, you can regain control over your spending habits, making informed choices that align with your financial goals and values. This empowerment puts you firmly in the driver's seat.

Repeat After Me... That's Not In My Budget

Let's imagine we're weavers, crafting our financial destinies thread by thread. Yet, in this intricate work of art, there's one tool that often goes underestimated; our words. The way we communicate about money can have a profound impact on our financial well-being. of language is a transformative power while your finances. So, repeat after me: ***"That's not in my budget."*** It might seem simple, but the words we choose when discussing our finances hold incredible power. They reflect our intentions, shape our decisions, and influence the perceptions of those around us. When you declare, "That's not in my budget," you're not just uttering a phrase; you're making a statement about your financial priorities.

We're Not Broke, We're on a Budget

One common misconception, is that adhering to a budget equates to financial hardship. In reality, instead of viewing it as a restriction, embrace your budget as a plan, a strategy to ensure your money aligns with your priorities, and gets you to where you want to be. When someone extends an invitation or opportunity that threatens to derail your financial plan, proudly state that you're on a budget. It's not about being broke; it's about being focused. By confidently stating your commitment to your budget, you set boundaries that protect your financial future.

Ultimately, money is a tool, a means to an end, rather than an end itself. It flows through our lives, offering opportunities to support the things we value most. Whether it's building a secure future, investing in personal growth, or nurturing meaningful relationships, your financial choices should align with your true priorities. Your words can also inspire those around you. When friends and family witness your commitment to a budget-centric lifestyle, they may become inspired to take control of their finances as well.

Your budget becomes your ally, helping you toward a future where your money fuels what truly matters and your financial well-being thrives. So, repeat after me: "That's not in my budget."

Hitting The Brakes On The Swipe Happy Syndrome

In the age of digital wallets, contactless payments, and one-click shopping, it's easier than ever to succumb to what we'll call the "Swipe-Happy Syndrome." It's that impulse to swipe your card or tap your screen without a second thought, driven by convenience and instant gratification. While there's nothing wrong with embracing technology, it's essential to strike a balance between convenience and financial responsibility.

The Swipe-Happy Syndrome is a modern financial dilemma that affects people of all ages. It stems from the seamless integration of technology into our daily lives, making it effortless to make purchases with the tap of a finger or phone. Whether it's ordering takeout, shopping online, or subscribing to streaming services, one of the primary drivers of the Swipe-Happy Syndrome is the thrill of instant gratification. With a quick swipe or tap, you can have that trendy item, mouthwatering meal, or entertainment at your fingertips.

While the Swipe-Happy Syndrome provides immediate satisfaction, it often comes at a long-term cost. Repetitive spending can lead to overspending, credit card debt, and financial stress. Moreover, it may divert funds away from your long-term aspirations. One way to curb this craving is to remove stored payment methods from online shopping platforms and apps. Having to enter your payment details each time can create a pause for reflection. You can also begin to track your spending, small purchases tend to add up. This practice can provide insight into your spending patterns and reveal areas where you can cut back.

By implementing these strategies, you can regain control over the Swipe-Happy Syndrome and make more intentional spending choices. Remember, technology and convenience are wonderful tools, but they should serve your financial goals rather than derail them.

The Spending Commandments

In the world of personal finance, there are time-tested principles that guide us toward financial wisdom and stability. Let's delve into what we'll affectionately call "The Spending Commandments." While they may not have been chiseled onto stone tablets, they hold immense power in shaping our financial destinies. These are the sacred rules designed to help you keep your spending habits in check.

Know Thy Budget

Your budget isn't a restriction but a roadmap for financial success. Understanding your income and expenses ensures that your spending aligns with your financial goals

Honor Thy Financial Goals

Always stay committed to your long-term objectives. Whether it's saving for a home, building an emergency fund, or investing for retirement, your goals should guide your spending decisions.

Thou shalt not impulse buy

Resist the allure of spontaneous purchases. Instead, take a step back, consider the necessity of the item, and practice mindful spending.

Worry about thyself

In the era of social media, it's easy to compare ourselves to others and desire their lifestyles. focus on our own financial journey and not be swayed by appearances.

Keep A Spending Sabbath

Pause and reflect on your financial choices, and regain control over your impulses. This might look like "we got food at home," or inviting friends over for a night in (where they bring the potluck and you provide the streaming service you already pay for).

Thou Shalt Not Ignore Value

Seek value in your purchases. Consider the quality, durability, and long-term benefits of an item rather than solely its price.

Give unto Savings

Allocate a portion of your income to savings. It's a reminder that saving is not a luxury but a necessity for financial security.

Thou Shalt Not Waste Money on Fees

If you see a fee, always call and ask for a courtesy waiver of the fee. If the first rep says "no"... be kind, hang up, and call again. Call three times if you have to, speaking with even more kindness at each attempt.

Seek Wise Council

Consult experts or trusted individuals who can provide guidance on your financial journey. This can be friends, family, or a professional at your bank or in the community.

Thou Shalt Review Thy Finances Regularly

Regular financial check-ins help you track your progress, identify areas for improvement, and stay aligned with your financial goals.

It's essential to remember a fundamental truth that every purchase you make is a statement. It's a declaration of your values, priorities, and financial aspirations. Your spending choices carry the power to either propel you towards your financial goals or divert you from the path of financial success. However, as you've learned throughout this chapter, mindful spending is the key to financial empowerment. Every time you reach for your wallet or click the "Buy Now" button, take a moment to reflect. Ask yourself, "Does this purchase align with my financial goals?" Consider whether it brings you closer to your dreams or pulls you further away.

Your financial journey is unique, and your goals are worth pursuing. Your spending choices play a vital role in achieving these objectives. Each dollar spent wisely is a step closer to financial freedom. By making conscious spending decisions, you ensure that each purchase contributes to your goals.

So, as you navigate the world of spending, let your financial goals be your guiding star. Embrace "The Spending Commandments" curb impulse buying to honor your values and financial aspirations. Your financial story is still being written, every purchase is a statement that shapes it. Watch as your financial future becomes a reality.

Hmm.. do you really need it?

This worksheet provides an objective perspective on your potential purchases, helping to ensure that it's a wise and beneficial decision.

Do I need this item or do I just want it?

Will this purchase fulfill a basic necessity or is it for pleasure?

____

____

____

Do I need this item How often will I use this item?

Is it a one-time use or will it be used regularly?

____

____

____

Is the cost of the item justified by the value it provides?

Am I paying for quality or just for the brand?

____

____

____

Does this purchase fit within my current budget?

Will buying this now cause financial strain in the near future?

____

____

____

Is this a long-term investment or a short-term gratification?

Will this item hold its value over time?

____

____

____

Am I making this purchase on impulse or after careful consideration?

Am I buying this to feel better emotionally?

____

____

____

The Spending Spectrum

Rank your shopping desires by writing them in the segment that best corresponds with their importance.

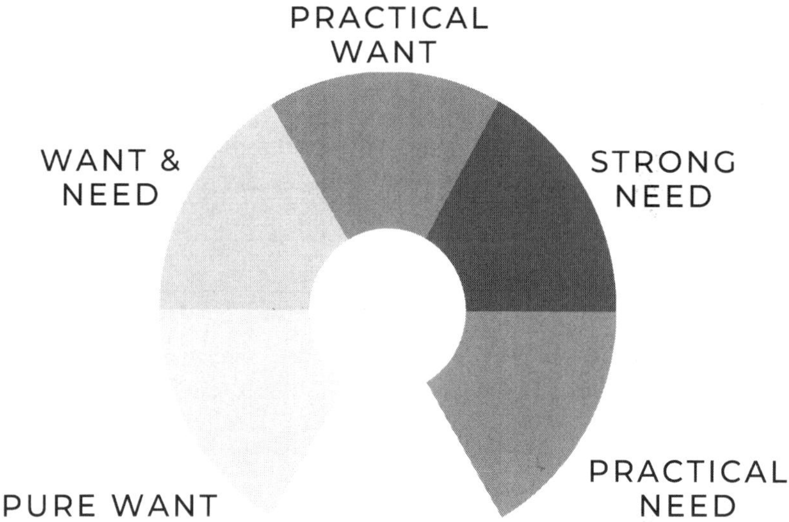

The Spending Personality Quiz

Unmasking Your Inner Shopaholic

When you receive your paycheck, what's your first thought?

A. Pay bills and save whatever is left.
B. Plan a major purchase or a night out.
C. Save a portion, and spend a little.
D. Paycheck? I'm already planning my next shopping spree!

How do you feel about budgeting?
A. I stick to my budget religiously.
B. I try to budget, but it's not strict.
C. Budgeting is necessary, but I can be flexible.
D. Budget? What's that?

What prompts you to shop?
A. Only when I need something specific.
B. Sales and special deals.
C. When I'm feeling emotional or want to reward myself.
D. Anytime. I love shopping!

How do you feel after making a big purchase?
A. Content, if it was planned and within budget.
B. Excited, but sometimes a bit guilty.
C. Mixed feelings. It depends on the purchase.
D. Thrilled! I can't wait for the next big buy.

How often do you impulse buy?
A. RARELY, IF EVER.
B. Occasionally, if it's a good deal.
C. Fairly often, especially if I'm stressed.
D. All the time– it's a habit.

Do you research before buying an expensive item?
A. Always– I compare prices and check reviews.
B. Usually, unless it's a limited-time offer.
C. Sometimes, but it's not my top priority.
D. Research? I go with my gut feeling.

What's your approach to sales and discounts?

A. Useful for items I was already planning to buy.
B. Tempting, but I try to be cautious.
C. Hard to resist, I end up buying things I didn't plan to.
D. I love sales! More items for less money!

How do you handle credit cards?

A. I use them carefully and pay off the balance promptly.
B. I use them, but sometimes struggle to pay in full.
C. I rely on them often and worry about the debt.
D. Credit cards are my best friends for shopping sprees.

This quiz can be a fun and insightful way for you to reflect on your spending habits and consider areas where you can improve your financial health.

Flip for answers!

Mostly A's: The Budget Master

You're a pro at managing your finances. Shopping is more about necessity than pleasure for you.

Mostly B's: The Cautious Shopper

You enjoy shopping but are aware of your limits. You try to balance pleasure with practicality.

Mostly C's: The Emotional Spender

Your spending is often influenced by your emotions. You might make impulsive purchases but are somewhat aware of the consequences.

Mostly Ds: The Born Shopaholic

Shopping is a significant part of your life. You love the thrill of it, but be cautious of overspending and accumulating debt.

Chapter Two

You Got Money For That?

Picture this - You're giving main character energy but your wallet is not the Tia to your Tamera. It's time to set the stage for financial success!

Meet Lily, the Trendy Twenty-Something who splurged on a shopping spree only to realize she's gonna be broke till payday. Talk about a spending problem. Lily had a job, a modest apartment, and a group of friends who were always up for a night out on the town. With a paycheck that arrived like clockwork every other week, money, it seemed, was no longer that tightrope she had to walk in college. It was her ticket to the world, to those stylish boutiques that beckoned her, and to the Instagram-worthy brunch spots her friends adored. Our story opens in her charming, urban-chic apartment on a bright Sunday morning. The aftermath of her latest shopping spree playfully scattered around. Amidst the trendy bags and latest outfits, Lily experienced a moment of clarity. It dawned on her that while she loved the thrill of new purchases, she yearned for a more balanced and mindful approach to spending. With her cat, Ziggy, purring beside her, she pulled out a newly bought, brightly colored budget planner. Its pages were untouched, inviting her to start a fresh chapter. She started writing, categorizing her expenses, and outlining her budget, Lily felt a growing sense of empowerment. She realized that managing her finances isn't just about constraint; it's about making choices that reflect her values and goals.

In the daily chaos of life, it's easy to let our financial goals and dreams take a back seat. Bills need to be paid, emergencies demand attention, and the temptation to treat yourself after a hard day can lure us away from long-term aspirations. There's no better time to pause and define what financial success means to you. This is where your financial clarity comes in.

Budget Is Not A Bad Word

What are finances?

Finances are the monetary resources and affairs of a country, organization, or person. When it comes to your finances, having a clear sense of what you want to achieve is the first step towards making your dreams a reality. It's like setting coordinates for a thrilling journey; without them, you might end up lost and aimless.

So, what do you want to accomplish? Do you dream of a comfortable home filled with everything you need? Are you passionate about supporting causes close to your heart? Perhaps you aspire to start your own business or travel the world. The beauty of financial goals is that they can be as unique as your fingerprint.

Financial goals come in two flavors: short-term and long-term.

Short-term goals are like the appetizers of your financial journey- quick wins that help you see you're on the right track and keep you motivated. Long-term goals are the main course, they require patience, discipline, and a sprinkle of delayed gratification. They might include building an emergency fund, paying off a credit card, or taking a dream vacation. They're the goals you can achieve in the next few months or years.

Long-term goals are the grand visions that paint the canvas of your life. They could involve buying a house, funding your children's education, or achieving financial independence. These goals take time, careful planning, and usually involve substantial investments. Now that you've pondered your aspirations, it's time to turn those dreams into tangible targets. Let's make it real! Break down your goals into SMART goals.

SMART GOALS

Specific	Clearly define what you want to achieve. Instead of saying, "I want to save money," specify, "I want to save $5,000 for a down payment on a car."
Measurable	Establish a concrete metric to track your progress. For example, "I will save $500 per month for 10 months."
Achievable	Ensure that your goal is realistic and attainable within your current financial situation.
Relevant	Make sure your goals align with your values and priorities. It's about pursuing what truly matters to you.
Time bound	Set a deadline for when you want to achieve your goal. This adds a sense of urgency and helps you stay on track.

Why Budgeting Is for Everybody (especially you!)

Budgeting- it's a word that might conjure images of spreadsheets, number crunching, and financial restraint. You might be thinking, "Is this really for me? Do I need a budget?" The resounding answer is yes, and I'm here to tell you why. Contrary to popular belief, it isn't reserved for financial gurus. A budget is a tool that can empower anyone, including you, to make the most of their money. Think of it as your financial GPS, telling your money where it should go. Also, a budget isn't all about restricting, Author Tiffani Aliche looks at a budget as a 'say yes' plan,' it helps you figure out how to get the things you want.

At the core, budgeting is all about understanding your cash flow. It's about knowing where your money comes from, where it goes, and how it behaves along the way. Your income is the star of the show, but your expenses, both fixed and variable, have supporting roles that can either make or break the performance. Let me break it down a bit more.

Your income is the money you earn from various sources, such as your job, investments, or side hustles. It's the cash you have to work with, the foundation upon which your financial story is built. Expenses on the other hand are the cost of living your life, and they come in three main categories:

Fixed Expenses
These are the consistent bills you pay regularly, like rent or mortgage, utilities, and loan payments. They play the role of steady supporting actors, always present, and you can predict their lines.

Variable Expenses
These include groceries, entertainment, dining out, and other flexible costs that can vary from month to month.

Periodic Expenses
These are the expenses that only come up a few times a year, holiday meals, travel to see loved ones, gifts and special occasions. ***This is the category that gets the least love in budgeting.***

Picture your cash flow as the narrative of your financial life. It starts with your income taking the stage and setting the scene for the month. As the month unfolds, your expenses enter, each one playing its part. The sweet spot is when your income can cover the expenses and leave room for saving, investing, and fun. Now, here's where budgeting comes in. With a well-crafted budget, you can:

- **Plan Ahead:** Anticipate your income and expenses for the month.
- **Track Progress:** Monitor your spending to ensure you stay on track with your financial goals.
- **Make Informed Choices:** Budgeting empowers you to make informed decisions about where your money goes, ensuring that your priorities take center stage.
- **Build Savings:** Allocate a portion of your income to savings and investments, nurturing the growth of your financial future.

In essence, It's not about restriction or deprivation; it's about *empowerment and control.* With a budget in hand, you become the director of your financial story, making sure it's a masterpiece filled with financial success. So, is budgeting for everybody? Absolutely, and especially for you. It's the key to ensuring that your money is working for you, not against you. Now let's delve deeper into the art of budgeting, equipping you with the tools and knowledge to master this essential financial skill.

Understanding Cashflow

In the intricate dance of personal finance, understanding the dynamic duo of inflows and outflows is crucial. These financial forces shape the tides of your monetary existence, determining whether you sail smoothly or find yourself navigating choppy waters.

Inflows encompass all the sources of money flowing into your life, replenishing your financial well. Here are some common examples of inflows:

- **Salary:** The primary source for many, your salary represents the money you earn from your job.
- **Side Hustles:** Income generated from side gigs or freelance work adds to your financial inflow.
- **Investments:** Earnings from investments, such as dividends, interest, or capital gains, contribute to your financial health.
- **Gifts and Windfalls:** Unexpected cash, like a birthday gift or a tax refund, also fall into this category.
- **Rental Income:** If you own property, the rent you receive is part of your inflow.
- **Business Profits:** If you're an entrepreneur, your business's profits can be a significant source of inflow.

Understanding your inflows means having a clear picture of how much money you have at your disposal. It's the starting point for effective financial planning.

On the flip side, **outflows** represent where your money goes. These are the financial commitments, obligations, and choices that shape your daily life. Common outflows include:

- **Bills and Utilities:** Rent or mortgage payments, electricity, water, and other essentials.
- **Groceries and Household Expenses:** The costs of feeding yourself and maintaining your home.
- **Transportation:** Expenses related to commuting, car payments, or public transportation.
- **Debt Repayments:** Credit card bills, loans, and other debt obligations.
- **Entertainment and Lifestyle:** Dining out, delivery service, leisure activities, and personal indulgences.
- **Irregular or occasional expenses:** Birthday gifts, holiday meals, contributions to a friend or family member in need.
- **Savings and Investments:** Allocating funds towards savings accounts or investments.

Understanding your outflows is equally vital. It's about knowing where your money is committed and how it's distributed among various aspects of your life. Your financial equilibrium rests on the delicate balance between inflows and outflows. When your inflows exceed your outflows, you have room to save, invest, and work toward your financial goals.

On the other hand, when outflows outweigh inflows, it can lead to financial stress, debt, and a lack of progress toward your dreams. Budgeting ensures that your inflows are allocated efficiently among your outflows. With a well-crafted budget, you can Allocate resources to what matters most to you, whether it's building an emergency fund, paying off debt, or saving for a dream vacation. Knowing where your money goes ensures that your finances remain on course. Tracking your money offers a plethora of benefits. It puts you in the driver's seat of your financial journey, allowing you to make informed decisions about your money, while providing a clear view of your spending habits, allowing you to identify areas where you can cut costs or reallocate funds.

Daily Check-In: Set aside a few minutes each day to review your spending. You can do this in the morning or before bed. I personally prefer the morning, my mind is clearer when I don't have a stressful money dream.

Record Expenses: Log all your expenses, whether it's a cup of coffee or a significant purchase. Be thorough, there are tons of apps that can help with this so you don't have to track using pen and paper.

Categorize: Assign each expense to a category (e.g., groceries, entertainment, utilities).

Review, Reflect, and Adjust: At the end of the week, take a moment to review your spending. Are there any surprises or areas where you exceeded your budget? If you notice that you're consistently overspending in a specific category, adjust your budget accordingly for the following week or month reallocate funds.

Pro Tip

If you use one debit or credit card for most of your expenses, your bank is already doing the tracking for you!

Financial tracking isn't a one-time exercise; it's a lifestyle. Cultivating an awareness of your money's movements makes it easier to make corrections and adjustments. Over time, this practice becomes second nature, just part of what you do.

Anticipating Future Income and Expenses

Imagine having a crystal ball that reveals your financial future-the ability to foresee upcoming income and expenses with clarity and confidence. While I can't provide you with a mystical orb, I can equip you with the next best thing: the art of anticipating future income and expenses. Let's dive into the crystal-clear waters of financial foresight, enabling you to navigate your financial journey with grace and preparedness. Here's why it's crucial.

Having financial foresight enables you to plan for upcoming financial needs, whether it's paying bills, saving for a vacation, or investing for retirement. Anticipation puts you in control of your finances, reducing the stress of financial surprises and ensuring that you have the funds ready to make progress toward your financial goals. If you keep track of what you save each month, you can project how much you'll have saved by the end of the year or in a few years.

Anticipating future income and expenses is the heart of financial planning. It's about being proactive, not reactive in managing your finances. Anticipating future income involves knowing when, how much, and from where you'll receive money. You also need to know what upcoming financial obligations you have. A solid, workable budget is the tool that helps you align your financial resources with your goals and obligations.

Subscription Scrutiny

In the age of subscription services, it's easy for your monthly expenses to sneak up on you. Netflix, Spotify, Amazon Prime, gym memberships, and that quirky snack box you signed up for during a midnight online shopping spree—all these subscriptions can silently nibble away at your budget.

First, let's acknowledge the elephant in the room—subscriptions are everywhere. They offer convenience, entertainment, and tailored experiences, but they can also become budget busters when left unchecked. The key to financial well-being is not necessarily slashing every subscription but examining them with a discerning eye. Think of subscriptions as small holes in your financial boat. Individually, they might not seem like a big deal, but when you have a dozen or more, they can lead to significant financial stress. To combat this, make a list of every subscription you're currently paying for and evaluate the value of each one. Are you getting your money's worth? Do you use it regularly, or has it become a digital relic? Sometimes, multiple subscriptions offer similar services. Do you really need three music streaming services, or can you consolidate?

Next, review your bank or credit card statements for any recurring charges you might have forgotten. These could be trial periods that turned into paid subscriptions (which surprisingly happens A LOT). Lastly, investigate whetherthere are free alternatives to the services you're paying for. Sometimes, you might find equally good options without the cost through your local library, an alumni association, or even your employer. As you scrutinize your subscriptions, consider whether they are Essential vs. Non-Essential.

Differentiate between subscriptions you truly need (like essential software for work) and those that are more for entertainment. If you use a subscription daily or weekly, it's likely more valuable than the one you use once in a blue moon. Subscription scrutiny isn't a one-time event; it's a lifestyle. Just as you maintain your car or home, you should routinely review your subscriptions. Consider doing a quarterly or annual subscription checkup to ensure you're only paying for what genuinely enhances your life. You'll save money and regain control over your budget.

So, what are you waiting for? Pull out that phone and get started on trimming the fat from your reoccurring expenses and directing your hard-earned coins toward the things that truly matter.

Needs, Wants & Wishes

Let's take a deep dive into the art of allocation and guide you through the intricacies of budgeting, and helping you craft a budget blueprint that distinguishes between your needs, wants, and wishes. Allocation is the process of dividing your financial resources among various categories, ensuring that each one gets its rightful share. Budgeting allocates your money to different areas of your life, each with its own purpose. Creating a budget is like designing the blueprint for your financial future. It begins with recognizing the hierarchy of your financial priorities. Take a look at the following:

Needs
These are essential expenses that are non-negotiable for daily living. They include items like rent or mortgage payments, utilities, groceries, and transportation costs. Needs are the foundation of your budget.

Wants
Wants encompass discretionary spending- things you desire but can live without. This category includes dining out, entertainment, fashion splurges, and hobbies. Fulfilling your wants should be balanced with your needs.

Wishes
Wishes are your financial dreams and goals. These are the long-term aspirations that drive your financial decisions, such as buying a home, traveling the world, or achieving financial independence. Wishes require dedicated savings and planning.

Allocate Your Financial Resources

Cover Your Needs

Allocate enough of your income to cover your essential needs. This ensures that your basic living expenses are consistently met with a small cushion so you have wiggle room when an unexpected cold front has you turning on the heat in June.

Balance your Wants

Allocate a portion of your budget to your wants, but do so judiciously. This category allows you to enjoy life's pleasures without overindulgence. Holding yourself too strict for too long isn't good either. *Build enjoyment into your budget.*

Invest in Your Wishes

Allocate a significant portion of your budget to fund your wishes. This involves saving and investing in your long-term goals, whether it's buying a house, retiring comfortably, or starting a business.

Keep in mind budgeting isn't just about planned expenses; it's also about preparing for the unexpected. Make sure you have these categories on your budget plan as well.

Emergency Fund - Allocate part of your budget to build and maintain an emergency fund. This financial cushion safeguards you from unforeseen circumstances like medical bills or car repairs.

Contingency Planning - Consider allocating a portion of your budget to contingency planning. This involves anticipating future expenses or life changes, like higher education or growing your family.

Modern budgeting is easier than ever thanks to an array of digital tools and apps. These tools can help you track your expenses, set budgeting goals, and monitor your financial progress. Incorporating such tools into your budgeting strategy can enhance your financial management.

Pro Tip

Use one account for all expenses over 2-3 months to see what your spending habits are in one place.

Remember, your budget isn't a static document; it's a dynamic tool that should adapt to your evolving financial situation and priorities. Regularly review and adjust your budget to stay aligned with your goals. By crafting a budget blueprint that clearly distinguishes between your needs, wants, and wishes, you'll gain control over your financial journey. You'll ensure that your spending aligns with your values and aspirations, paving the way for a more financially secure and fulfilling future.

Balancing Essentials, Fun, and Future

In the world of budgeting, simplicity is often the key to success. Let's build your budget. We aren't prescribing any ***50/30/20 or 90/10 rules.*** For you, we're simply figuring out where your money is actually coming and going. Until you know how you are using the money you have now, it would be foolish for us to give you some out-of-touch ratio to follow. We don't know your life! But also, *you might not either.*

Budgeting rules to stick by
1. Don't go over budget
2.Repeat rule #1

1. Calculate Your Net Income. Start with your after-tax income, which is what you take home after deductions like taxes, healthcare, life insurance, and retirement contributions.

2. Fill out the budget sheet based on how you spent money last month and the month before.

3. Ask yourself, do I have any expenses coming up that might not fit neatly into fixed or variable expenses? Do I have any celebrations that might require a new outfit or gift? Do I have a bill that I usually pay once a year like my car inspection or renewal of a software? Am I traveling for any reason?

Money Mantras

Money mantras are like affirmations for your financial well-being. They provide clarity by distilling complex financial concepts into simple, memorable phrases. Mantras also help you stay focused on your financial goals and values while also rewiring your brain to a positive money mindset about money, empowering you to make wise financial decisions.

Let's get crafty

Creating your money mantras is a personalized process. Start by reflecting on your financial goals, values, and challenges. What financial principles resonate with you? Here are a few examples to inspire your own mantras:

- **Spend mindfully, save intentionally:** This mantra encourages you to think before making purchases and to prioritize savings.
- **Debt is a tool or a burden:** you decide which based on how you use debt. It reminds you that it's important to approach borrowing with careful consideration and planning.
- **Invest in yourself, it pays the best interest:** Prioritizing personal growth and education can be a valuable investment.
- **Small steps lead to big financial victories:** This mantra emphasizes the power of consistent, incremental progress.

Some of my Faves

- Money is fun
- It's not in my budget
- My plan is working for me
- I control my money; my money does not control me
- I embrace abundance; there is always enough to go around
- I am the CEO of my financial life, I make strategic decisions for my wealth
- What I appreciate, appreciates. I am grateful for everything I have and everything that's coming to me

Once you've crafted your money mantras, incorporate them into your daily life. Start your day or end your night by reciting your money mantras. This sets a positive tone for your financial decisions.

As you journey through these chapters money mantras will be your constant companions. Whether you're budgeting, investing, saving, or giving, your mantras will remind you of your financial values and goals. Better yet, money mantras get the people around you to help you with your goals even if they repeat one of your mantras to you with an eye roll, *"We know, we know... it's not in your budget."*

Now imagine this, you're at your favorite cafe with a caramel latte in one hand and a budget planner in the other, diving into your monthly budgeting. Remember, your budget is your passport to a financially stable life.

"It's not how much money you make, but how much money you keep, how hard it works for you, and how many generations you keep it for."

-Robert Kiyosaki

Progress Tracker

Write a goal in each spot. Color each spot in when you reach the corresponding milestone.

Use this worksheet to map out your budget.

Monthly Budget

MONTH

VARIABLE / OTHER EXPENSES			
Date	Description	Notes	Amount

SAVINGS				
Account	Name	Starting Balance	Amount	End Balance

TOTALS	
Total Income	
Minus fixed expenses	
Minus savings	
Left for variable expenses	
End Balance	

The Ultimate Finance Tracker

Education	
DATE	AMOUNT

Travel	
DATE	AMOUNT

Gifts	
DATE	AMOUNT

Personal Spending	
DATE	AMOUNT

Chapter Three
Other People's Money

I knew Dayna from college, she was a few years younger but we were in some of the same student groups and kept in touch from time to time. We started spending more time together when we both ended up living in her hometown after graduate school. At the time, Dayna was working a job outside of her training because the expensive graduate degree she earned failed to pay returns on the investment. She's a go-getter and has always been financially responsible —even when graduate school and low-paying jobs made it all but impossible to keep debt down.

After graduate school the credit cards that kept her afloat during unpaid internships and long, unreimbursed commutes to experiential classes were now sinking her ship. One day, as Dayna was scrolling through her email, a particularly dreaded message popped up: the monthly credit card statement.

Normally, she glanced at the balance, paid the minimum due, and moved on. But this time, something was different. The balance seemed larger, more ominous, and the minimum payment barely made a dent. Dayna's heart raced as she dug deeper into the statement. She realized that her once manageable credit card balances had ballooned into a formidable beast of high-interest debt. Her purchases of late-night study snacks, gas, and groceries had added up over time.

In a state of mild panic, Dayna decided to take a closer look at her credit card statements from the past few months. She couldn't believe her eyes—interest charges, late fees, and cash advance fees had gnawed away at her hard-earned money. The very tools that helped her survive what she thought was temporary brokenness in grad school had ensnared her in a web of financial stress. As Dayna sat down at her desk, surrounded by her spreadsheets and color-coded budgeting tools, trying to figure out how her expenses were relatively low, and her salary was decent but she was still living paycheck to paycheck. She reached out and we crafted a plan like the one we'll go over in this chapter, to simplify the tracking of her accounts, and to leverage a lump sum payment she was expecting to get headway on her debt.

> "Remember, darling, credit isn't just a card; it's trust, hard-earned and held in high regard."
>
> *-Anonymous*

The Good, The Bad and All That Jazz

While we all aspire to be so detached from debt that we pronounce the b like tennis champion Coco Gauff, most of us aren't so lucky. Debt—it's a word that can evoke both anxiety and opportunity, depending on how you manage it. In this chapter, we're going to unravel the intricate world of debt, exploring the good, the bad, and all the financial jazz that comes with it. So, let's decipher the complexities of debt, including the critical concept of the debt-to-income ratio and the nuances of purchasing a home. Debt is a financial tool that, when used wisely, can facilitate wealth-building and economic advancement. Understanding your debt-to-income ratio, distinguishing between good and bad debt, and making informed decisions about financing significant investments like a home, are pivotal steps on your financial journey.

How to Leverage Borrowing to Boost Your Finances

There's a debt side that's often overlooked—a side that can be harnessed for creating wealth and financial empowerment. It's time to shift your perspective from viewing debt as a burden to recognizing it as an opportunity. Good debt isn't a myth; it's a strategic financial move. It involves borrowing money to make it work for you, rather than against you. The wealth-building potential of good debt stems from its ability to facilitate investments that appreciate or generate income over time.

One of the most iconic examples of good debt is a mortgage. Owning a home financed through a mortgage can be a pathway to substantial wealth accumulation. While the monthly mortgage payments may seem like an expense, they're, in fact, an investment. Real estate has historically appreciated over time, making your home not just a place to live but also a valuable asset. As property values increase, your home's equity grows, adding to your net worth. In essence, you're leveraging borrowed money to acquire an asset that has the potential to appreciate significantly, especially over the long term.

Education loans, often associated with the pursuit of higher education, represent an investment in yourself. When used wisely, these loans enable you to acquire knowledge, skills, and qualifications that can open doors to higher-paying job opportunities. This type of borrowing is a strategic move to boost your earning potential. Consider it an investment in your future earnings. The income you generate with your enhanced skills can more than offset the cost of borrowing. It's an example of good debt that aligns with the concept of investing in yourself. Investors understand the power of leveraging borrowed funds to grow their investment portfolios. Whether it's investing in stocks, bonds, or real estate, the use of investment loans can magnify the returns on your investments.

One example I like to give in coaching sessions is the up and coming landlord with $150,000 cash to purchase a home to rent out. With that $150,000 this investor could buy one house out right and collect $1,500 in rent or they could buy five homes with a 20% down payment, collect $2,850 in rent each month after paying the mortgages on the five properties.

Scenario 1:
Buy Home for $150,000 with cash
Home Price = $150,000
Rent Collected = $1,500/month
Revenue = $18,000 per year

Scenario 2: Borrow to Buy Five Houses
Each Home Price = $150,000
Down payment required for each home = $30,000
Mortgage payment for each home = $930/month
(assuming $120,000 mortgage at 7% for 30 years) x5
= $4,650
Rent collected = $7,500 per month
Revenue = $34,000 per year

This type is a prime example of good debt in action because the returns on your investments outpace the cost of borrowing. While the potential for wealth creation through good debt is enticing, it's essential to approach borrowing with careful consideration and planning.

Here are some key factors to bear in mind:

- Interest Rates: Seek out favorable interest rates when taking on debt. Lower rates reduce the overall cost of borrowing, making it easier to generate a positive return on your investment.

- Financial Planning: Develop a comprehensive financial plan that includes debt management as a strategic component. Ensure that you can comfortably meet your debt obligations while pursuing your financial goals.

- Credit Management: Maintain a strong credit history and credit score. A positive credit profile can help you access better loan terms and lower interest rates.

- Diversification: Avoid over concentration in any single asset or form of debt. Diversifying your investments and debt portfolio can enhance your financial resilience.

"Good credit is more than a score; it's a door to so much more."
-Anonymous

The wealth-building potential of good debt is undeniable. It's a tool that, when used wisely, can propel your financial standing to new heights. Mortgages, education loans, business loans, and investment loans all have the power to enhance your wealth when approached strategically. By shifting our perspective from fearing debt to leveraging it for financial empowerment, we unlock opportunities for long-term prosperity and financial security. Good debt is not a financial monster, it's an ally on your journey to wealth and financial success.

Balancing Debt for Your Financial Future

Debt is a liability in technical terms, but it can help you build your assets depending on how it's managed and utilized. Achieving the right balance involves understanding the types of debt you carry, their purposes, and their impact on your overall financial health. Your debt-to-income ratio is an essential metric that calculates the percentage of your income that goes toward debt repayment each month. It's a crucial tool for lenders when determining your creditworthiness. To calculate your debt-to-income ratio, add up all your monthly debt payments- mortgage or rent, credit card bills, student loans, car loans, and any other debts. Then, divide this total by your monthly gross income (your income before taxes). Multiply the result by 100 to express it as a percentage. For instance, if your total monthly debt payments amount to $1,500, and your gross monthly income is $5,000, your debt-to-income ratio would be 30%. Lenders typically prefer a debt-to-income ratio below 43% to consider you a safe bet for lending.

Borrowers with a DTI below 36% have an easier time getting loans with favorable rates. If you carry high-interest debt, like credit card balances, prioritize paying it down aggressively. High-interest debt can quickly spiral out of control, consuming a significant portion of your income. When considering new debt, evaluate the purpose, value, and potential return on investment of the purchase.

Good debt should align with your financial goals and have a clear strategy for generating returns. If you use debt to invest, diversify your investments to spread risk. Avoid concentrating your investments on a single asset class. Balancing debt requires financial literacy and discipline. Understanding the terms of your loans, managing interest rates, and creating a repayment plan are essential components of effective debt management. Moreover, making informed decisions about borrowing and investment can prevent. you from falling into a debt trap.

Not all debt is created equal, and understanding the distinction between good debt and bad debt is essential for making informed financial decisions. Good debt is debt that has the potential to increase your net worth or improve your financial future. It's an investment rather than an expense. Some examples of good debt include student loans, mortgages, or even business loans. Conversely, bad debt is debt that does not contribute to your financial well-being and often leads to financial strain. Examples of bad debt include credit card debt, payday loans, and car title loans.

One of the most significant financial decisions many individuals make is purchasing a home. It's a milestone that often involves substantial borrowing. The dream of homeownership is deeply ingrained in the American psyche. It's often seen as a symbol of financial stability and success. However, the path to owning a home involves making a series of important financial decisions, and one of the most crucial is how to finance it.

For most individuals, purchasing a home involves taking out a mortgage—a type of secured loan specifically designed for buying real estate. Mortgages come in various forms, but the most common ones are fixed-rate and adjustable-rate mortgages (ARMs).

With a fixed-rate mortgage, your interest rate remains the same throughout the life of the loan. This provides stability and predictability in your monthly payments, making it easier to budget.

ARMs on the other hand, have an initial fixed-rate period, after which the interest rate can adjust periodically based on market conditions. While ARMs often start with lower interest rates, they can become riskier if rates rise significantly. Some individuals may consider alternative forms of debt, such as personal loans or lines of credit, to finance a home. While these options can be viable, they come with their own terms, interest rates, and considerations. It's essential to thoroughly research and understand all of these alternatives before pursuing them.

Purchasing a home is a significant financial decision that shapes your future. If you are thinking about buying a home, look for free homebuyer education programs in your area, check with the state housing authority, Habitat for Humanity, the United Way (211.org), and findhelp.org. These programs not only help you understand the financials of buying and owning a home, but many include a basics of home maintenance training and may even give you access to down payment assistance or repair/ rehabilitation grants. Homeownership is still the centerpiece of the American dream so in chapter 9 "Look At You Adulting!" we'll talk about ways you can decide when renting vs buying is the best fit for your values and goals.

Breaking Up With Debt

When debt is draining your resources and limiting your options, it's time to tap into the strategies below to kick debt to the curb and regain control of your financial future. Whether it's credit card debt, personal loans, or other forms of consumer debt, the first step to liberation is acknowledging its presence, writing down every dollar you owe to anybody (yes, even the $30 you borrowed from your cousin in 2022), then pulling up your sleeves to make and follow a debt reduction plan. ***Refer to The Debt Tracker Sheet at the end of this chapter.*** Once you have written down all your debts, decide whether you are going to snowball or avalanche.

Snowball vs. Avalanche: Unveiling the Art of Paying Off Debt Like a Pro

Imagine a snowball rolling down a hill, gaining size and momentum. That's the essence of ***the snowball method***, a debt repayment strategy that focuses on small victories to build motivation. Here's how it works:

1. Take the debts you put on the tracker, then reorder them from the smallest to the largest, regardless of interest rates.

2. Attack the Smallest Debt First: Make minimum payments on all your debts except the smallest one. Devote any extra funds you can muster to paying off this debt as quickly as possible.

3. Celebrate Small Wins: As you pay off each debt, celebrate your victory. This psychological boost keeps you motivated and engaged in the debt repayment process.

4. Snowball Effect: Once the smallest debt is gone, take the money you were putting towards it and apply it to the next smallest debt. This creates a snowball effect, where your payments get larger and more impactful as you progress.

The Snowball method may not save you the most money on interest, but it's incredibly effective at keeping you engaged and motivated. Small wins along the way provide a sense of accomplishment.

Now, picture an avalanche thundering down a mountainside, clearing everything in its path. ***The Avalanche method*** is like that—focused, strategic, and efficient. Here's how it works:

1. Like the Snowball method, take the debts you listed on the tracker but this time, arrange them by interest rate, from the highest to the lowest.

2. Attack the Highest Interest Debt First: Make minimum payments on all your debts except the one with the highest interest rate.

3. Interest Savings: As you eliminate high-interest debt, you save more on interest charges compared to the Snowball method.

4. Repeat the Process: Once the highest interest debt is gone, move on to the next highest, and so on. Your debt-clearing momentum builds as you tackle each high-interest obligation.

The avalanche method is like a precise financial strike. It may not offer the same emotional victories as the snowball method, but it saves you the most money in interest charges over time.

So, *Snowball or Avalanche?* Deciding between the two methods depends on your financial personality. Are you someone who thrives on quick wins and motivation, even if it means paying a bit more in interest? Then the Snowball method may be your choice. But if you're a numbers-driven, financially strategic individual who wants to save the most money in the long run, the Avalanche method might be yours. Whichever method you choose, the crucial step is to start. Make a plan, stick to it, and watch your debt dwindle as your financial freedom grows. Whether it's the Snowball's small victories or the Avalanche's efficiency, the art is in your commitment.

To accelerate debt repayment, consider increasing your income. This could involve taking on a part-time job, freelancing, or pursuing side gigs. The additional income can be channeled directly into paying off your debts. Then, develop a comprehensive budget that outlines your monthly expenses and discretionary spending. By scrutinizing your spending habits, you can identify areas where you can cut back and allocate more funds toward debt repayment. Don't be shy... Contact your creditors and inquire about the possibility of lowering your interest rates. A reduced interest rate can significantly decrease the cost of servicing your debt.

You can also explore debt consolidation options, such as transferring high-interest credit card balances to a lower-interest card or consolidating multiple loans into a single, more manageable payment. Getting rid of debt isn't just about the financial benefits; it's also about the freedom it brings. You will feel a reduction of financial stress and the money you were once channeling toward debt payments can now be redirected into savings and investments. Managing debt responsibly can also boost your credit score, improving your access to favorable financial products and interest rates.

A win is a win : How starting small can lead to big financial triumphs

The road to financial triumph often begins with modest steps- a seemingly inconsequential action that, over time, accumulates into something extraordinary. This journey is a testament to the profound impact of starting small, a practice that can ultimately lead to significant financial victories. Imagine a tiny seed planted in fertile soil. At first, it's barely noticeable, but with the right care, it grows into a mighty oak tree. Similarly, when dealing with finance, small actions taken consistently can yield remarkable results. Let's explore how starting small can pave the way for substantial financial triumphs. Starting small is not confined to debt repayment; it's equally potent in savings and investing.

Consider this: you aim to accumulate $2,500 for a down payment or emergency fund, a seemingly daunting task. Rather than being overwhelmed, you break it down into manageable increments:

- Save $100 this month.
- Trim an extra $50 from your monthly expenses.
- Allocate $300 from a tax refund.
- Generate $200 from side gigs.

These modest actions, akin to individual snowflakes, begin to accumulate. Over time, they coalesce into a financial snowstorm, propelling you toward your $2,500 goal. Each small step forward represents a victory worthy of celebration. Investing is yet another domain where starting small wields significant influence. Instead of feeling compelled to inject a substantial sum all at once, consider the power of gradual investment. This might involve setting up automatic contributions to your retirement accounts or investment portfolios, even if they start with modest amounts. The magic of incremental investing lies in its consistency. Through regular contributions and the alchemy of compound interest, small, regular investments can turn into substantial financial triumphs over time.

Celebrating small wins isn't about extravagant fanfare or indulgent splurges; it's about recognizing your progress, regardless of its magnitude. Here are some ways to mark your financial victories:

- Treat yourself to a modest indulgence, perhaps a favorite coffee or dessert.
- Maintain a "win jar" filled with notes documenting your achievements, read them during moments of wavering motivation.
- Share your successes with supportive friends or family who champion your financial aspirations.
- Remind yourself that a win is a win.

Embracing the concept of celebrating small wins can build momentum, sustain motivation, and guide you toward your financial objectives, one step at a time. Starting with small actions can ultimately lead to profound financial achievements. So, begin with the small, acknowledge each step, and witness the growth. Remember love, you're in control of your financial destiny. Let's make sure sure your debt story has an ending as amazing as you.

Payment Progress Tracker

Use this activity sheet to document your progress toward debt liberation.

CREDITOR ______________________ TARGET PAYOFF DATE ______________________

ACCOUNT NO ______________________ TYPE ______________________

START BALANCE ______________________ MINIMUM PAYMENT ______________________

CREDIT LIMIT ______________________ INTEREST RATE ______________________

BALANCE	MINIMUM PAYMENT	AMOUNT PAID	DATE PAID	CONFIRMATION

NOTES:

Chapter Four

Umbrella Ella Ella

Your savings are the key that unlocks the treasure chest of financial freedom. This isn't just money in the bank; it's security, power, and the sheer liberation of a safety net. Imagine being able to flip your hair, look challenges in the eye, and say, "Not today!" because you've got that financial cushion. It's that "F you money" that lets you gracefully walk away from anything that doesn't serve you. As your savings grow, that sense of liberation grows too. You're no longer dependent on credit or loans to cover unexpected expenses, and you gain the confidence to take charge of your financial destiny

Meet Ramon, a lively and optimistic recent college graduate who just landed his first job in the bustling city. Life was looking bright, and Ramon was ready to take on the world. Armed with his degree and a new found independence, he felt invincible. However, one summer afternoon ominous clouds, which weren't in the day's forecast, began gathering, darkening the cityscape. Within minutes the heavens opened up in a torrential downpour, catching Ramon off guard. He found himself at the epicenter of this sudden storm, without an umbrella or raincoat, his shoes squelching with every step. With no other option, he made a beeline for the nearest café. As he stepped in, leaving a trail of water behind him, Ramon was a sight: drenched from head to toe, hair sticking to his forehead, and clothes clinging to him.

As he tried to shake off the rain and reclaim some semblance of composure, he overheard a lively conversation at the next table. A group of friends were passionately discussing their spontaneous plans for the weekend—a last-minute escape to a picturesque mountain retreat. Ramon's heart tinged with envy. He had always dreamed of such impromptu escapades, but his current situation painted a stark contrast. The rainstorm, though unexpected, should have been manageable. But here he was, borrowing money from his parents for an Uber ride home. It hit him hard: he had meticulously planned for monthly bills and invested a little for future dreams, but had entirely overlooked the unpredictable. He had no rainy day fund.

That evening, as the rain pattered against his window, Ramon reflected on his vulnerability. Life, he realized, was filled with unforeseen showers, some literal and others metaphorical. While he had begun to save for his retirement through work, he had neglected the immediate uncertainties that life could throw his way. This soggy misadventure was his wake-up call, he understood that while ambitions and dreams are essential, it's equally crucial to be prepared for life's sudden storms. The rain had washed away his illusion of complete preparedness, leaving behind a resolve to build a robust rainy day fund.

Rain or Shine

Embracing the Power of Savings

Some days are crystal clear, with skies so blue and open roads ahead, mirroring the best financial times when your paycheck seems enough, and all bills are comfortably settled. But then there are days clouded by a medical emergency, unexpected car repairs, or even losing a job. Having savings is like owning a trusty umbrella, ensuring that whatever the weather, you remain unfazed.

It might seem counterintuitive to think of savings when everything is going smoothly. However, consider this, sunny days are the best times to prepare for the storms. When financial skies are clear, it's the optimal moment to build up your savings. with a steady income flow, consider diverting a part of your paycheck to saving consistently. This isn't just about preparing for bad times; it's also about leverage. Over time, these accumulated savings can earn interest which compounds, leading to your money working for you even when you're not actively adding to the pot.

Beyond the tangible benefits of savings, there's an emotional aspect that's often overlooked. Savings offer a sense of security, a peace of mind. Knowing that you have a safety net can drastically reduce financial stress. There's a tranquility in understanding that you're prepared. It's essential to remember that saving isn't about denying oneself but about prioritizing. When you are starting out (or starting over), it's deciding that the security of tomorrow holds more weight than the luxury of today.

> "In anticipation for precipitation stack chips for a rainy day."
> *-Jay Z*

A Savings State of Mind: Ensuring Financial Security

Financial security is also about the mindset you cultivate. At its core, saving isn't a mere financial act but a transformative way of thinking, one that prioritizes long-term prosperity over short-term gains. It's a profound commitment to one's future self, a recognition of the ephemeral nature of current wants compared to long-term needs. This state of mind is characterized by forward-thinking, patience, and an unwavering focus on enduring financial goals.

One of the cornerstones of a savings state of mind is understanding and practicing delayed gratification. It's the ability to resist the lure of an immediate reward in favor of a larger, more enduring benefit in the future. Think of it like this: foregoing that expensive coffee today might seem like a tiny sacrifice, but when compounded over time, it could amount to a significant sum in your savings account. Delayed gratification is also about making strategic choices and understanding that these decisions will yield significant returns in the long run. Transitioning from a spender to a saver requires more than just curbing expenses; it requires a fundamental shift in how you perceive money.

Money isn't just a means to satisfy current desires but a tool to forge a secure future. *To foster this shift* you must recognize your financial triggers. Understand what prompts you to spend. Is it emotional– perhaps retail therapy after a bad day? Or social– the pressure to keep up with peers? Recognizing these triggers is the first step to control them. Instead of seeing value in tangible purchases alone, consider the value of peace of mind that savings bring. A pricey gadget might offer temporary joy, but a robust emergency fund provides lasting security. Each time you resist a needless purchase or hit a savings milestone, celebrate it.

One of the most potent tools to strengthen a savings mindset is visualization. Picture your future – the home you want, the places you wish to travel, the security you aim to provide your family. These vivid mental images act as constant reminders of why you choose to save, making the process more purposeful. While cultivating the right mindset is vital, it's equally crucial to set up systems that facilitate savings. The more you learn about personal finance and the power of compound interest, the more motivated you'll be to save.

Even with a solid savings mindset, life can throw curve balls. An unexpected expense can disrupt your savings streak. However, instead of being disheartened, view these as temporary setbacks, not failures. The key is resilience–bouncing back, readjusting your plans, and continuing on your savings journey. A savings state of mind isn't cultivated overnight. It's a journey of understanding, discipline, and consistent commitment to future goals. However, once rooted, it transforms not just your bank balance but your entire approach to life. And that's a mindset worth investing in.

Emergency Funds: Your Financial Safety Net

Life is unpredictable. Just when you think you have everything figured out, unexpected events can turn your world upside down. These are realities many face, often without warning. It's for these unforeseen setbacks that an emergency fund is essential. It’s your financial safety net, ensuring you bounce back swiftly.

An emergency fund is a stash of money set aside to cover the financial surprises life throws your way. These unexpected events can be stressful, both emotionally and financially. By having an emergency fund, you ensure that money isn't an added stressor, granting you the mental space to handle the situation effectively. Without a safety net, people often turn to credit cards or loans to cover unexpected costs, plunging into debt. Additionally relying on friends or family during tough times can strain relationships. By having your own reserve, you maintain financial independence and control and reduce anxiety about the future.

While the exact amount to save varies based on individual circumstances, a general guideline is to have three to six months' worth of living expenses saved up. This ensures that even in prolonged emergencies, like a job loss, you have ample time to find a solution without compromising on your basic needs.

To be clear, we are NOT starting with three to six months. If you are starting or restarting your savings journey, we are first building the Oh! Sh*t fund. **An Oh! Sh*t fund** is $1,000 in a savings account. This is your immediate buffer against life's unexpected moments. It's not meant to cover all emergencies, but it will provide you with critical breathing room and buy you time to come up with a solution. After you have the OSF, then you start working towards these savings targets.

1st: $1000 OSF
2nd: One full month of expenses
3rd: Three months of expenses
4th: Six months of expenses

To build this up, you need to calculate how much you spend every month, including rent/mortgage, utilities, groceries, and other essentials. This gives you a clear target amount. Based on your expenses and income, determine how much you can comfortably set aside each month for your emergency fund. This account should be easily accessible, yet separate from your regular savings or checking account to avoid the temptation to dip into it. Review your monthly expenditures and see if there are non-essential items or services you can temporarily cut back on to boost your emergency savings.

Remember, this fund isn't for planned expenses like vacations or shopping sprees. Genuine emergencies are usually unforeseen, urgent, and necessary. Should you face an emergency and use part (or all) of your fund, prioritize rebuilding it. Reassess your budget, set a new savings goal, and work diligently to restore the safety net. The aim is always to be prepared. This financial buffer stands between you and potential debt, stress, and financial ruin.

It represents foresight, responsibility, and a commitment to your well-being. Building and maintaining an emergency fund requires discipline and sacrifice, but the peace of mind it brings is priceless.

How My Savings Showed Me I Made It

Growing up, a car issue could lead to a month of catch-up for the adults in my life. A breakdown meant missing work, a short paycheck or two, and then weeks of figuring out how to get things back on track, sometimes begging or borrowing help from a relative to close the gap, or simply going without. I remember when I was graduating college, and looking for a car, I was so hesitant to get a used car because of all the pent-up trauma I had around car breakdowns. Shortly after I moved to DC, I was running errands on a Saturday afternoon and had a dramatic blowout about a block from my apartment. I called a tow truck, and he let me know that the tire was beyond repair so he'd take me to a tire shop to get a replacement.

Because I'm always looking to keep more of my money in my pocket, I asked him to take me to the shop on the nearest military base, he told me he couldn't because they wouldn't let his truck on without a special tag but he knew a shop just off the base that had a good reputation for honest pricing. I reluctantly agreed. When he dropped me off at the shop, the technician let me know that I had to get a new tire and recommended that I get two new tires to prevent balance issues in the future. I did know he would recommend that because my uncle, who was a skilled 'hood mechanic", had given other people that same advice over the years. When he told me the amount for two tires, I took a deep breath and said "ok, but before I hand over my credit card, how much for four tires?

“I saw you had a buy two get two deal on your billboard.” He said, "Yes, I didn’t know if you’d be interested in that, two tires would be around $280 but four tires would be just about $100 more at $390.” I said that sounds like a better deal, so I’ll take four tires. I swiped my card and sat in the waiting area in nearly a cold sweat because I just spent $400 I hadn't planned to spend that day.

They changed the tires so quickly, that I didn’t even have a chance to ask if I could change my mind and go back to two. The tech handed me my keys and wished me well. I was a wreck walking to the car, thinking how could I spend that kind of money, what was I thinking, my car wasn’t very old, why did I need new tires? Then the moment of truth came, and I decided to drive off and try to fit in my last errand for the day.

As I pulled out of the parking lot, something almost magical happened, my car felt like it was brand new. Like brand new, the ride was smooth and quiet, and when I looked at the clock the whole ordeal didn’t even take two hours out of my day to solve. I remember almost tearing up in the car because something that was disastrous as a kid, had become just a minor inconvenience because I had money in my savings account for this unexpected expense. There was a new joy that washed over me when I drove myself in what felt like a new car.

The Cheat Code

When gearing up for a significant financial shift, like moving to a pricier apartment or upgrading your vehicle, it's essential to ensure your budget can withstand the change. Enter the financial "cheat code": a method to pressure test your budget before diving headfirst into larger commitments. The cheat code in finance lets you test your budget's capacity for upcoming expenses. Here's how it works:

Calculate the difference in cost between your current situation and the anticipated change. If your current rent is **$1,200** and you're eyeing an apartment that costs **$1,500,** the difference is **$300.** Instead of jumping directly into the new expense, start *"paying"* the difference into a savings account. Using the example above, you'd transfer $300 into savings every month, simulating the increased cost. Maintain this for four to six months. This cheat code allows you to:

1. **Pressure Test Your Budget:** Can your current income and spending habits accommodate the extra $300? If you find yourself constantly struggling, it's a clear sign you might not be ready for the upgrade.

2. **Build a Cushion:** By the end of six months, you'll have saved $1,800 (using the $300 example). This cushion can be useful for moving expenses, a down payment, or simply added to your emergency fund.

This exercise provides a tangible sense of how the upcoming change will affect your finances. It can help you decide whether to proceed, postpone, or reconsider. It cultivates a habit of setting aside money regularly and gives you a practice run with managing increased expenses. If you decide to move forward with your planned change, you have a tidy sum saved up to aid the transition. If not, you've simply grown your savings. A win is a win!

This method isn't just for housing transitions. Whether you're considering a car upgrade, thinking about starting a family, or any other significant financial shift, you can adapt this cheat code. The principle remains the same: *simulate the added expense a few months before you commit.*

The "cheat code" is a strategic way to mitigate potential financial strains by giving you a glimpse into the future. It's a proactive approach, ensuring that when you level up you're well-equipped to handle the challenges.

But FinanSis, where exactly do I get money to save?

Here's what matters about saving. If you are just starting, you need to find the amount of money, no matter how small, that you can consistently put away without missing it. Let me tell you why... let's say you decide to put $100 away each paycheck, but in between you find yourself pulling $40 here, $20 there, and another $30 out, psychologically, it's better to have the consistent success of putting away $10, over some time, you'll see your balance grow and will feel good about what you're doing, then you might say, maybe I can do $15 or $20 without noticing too much.

In the first chapter, I told you to figure out how much it cost you to live your life. Ok, so if you know how much you are spending on your day-to-day and month-to-month now, you might find opportunities to reduce those expenses:

1. Use coupons, discounts, and affiliations to reduce the cost of things you have to buy or like to buy. This can look a lot of ways, you don't have to go Extreme Couponer but you could:

- Plan your meals by checking the weekly ad at your favorite grocery store, or going to the restaurant you like on the day they have a special or discount.
- Search for coupon codes before you make any final purchases or use a cash-back app like ibotta, rakuten, getupside or one of the dozens of others that exist
- If you are a student, military dependent, or AAA member, ask if they have a discount, EVERYTIME.

2. Reduce temptation from email marketing, when you place orders or sign up for a store rewards program, have a completely different email address you use so you aren't bombarded with amazing opportunities to spend your money on things you probably don't need at 40% off. Help yourself keep 100% of your money. Try something such as firstname.rewards@favoriteemailservice.com. When you're ready to shop, you can ALWAYS go in and see when the retailer sent you a deal.

3. I'll say it in English and Spanish - There's food at home, hay comida en la casa. If you don't need it, don't buy it...no compras chingaderas

4. Check your subscriptions and memberships. The best way to really get money to dedicate to your financial goals, including savings, is to BOTH reduce your expenses and increase your income, we'll talk about the income part in chapter 8 "Minding the Business that Pays You!".

Exploring High-Yield Savings and Investment Accounts

In the financial world, letting money sit idle is a missed opportunity. With inflation nibbling away at your savings' purchasing power, it's crucial to explore avenues that can boost its growth. High-yield savings and investment options can be the key to preserving and enhancing your wealth.

Traditional savings accounts offer security, but their interest rates are often lackluster, barely outpacing inflation. Enter high-yield savings accounts, which provide considerably higher interest rates. The advantage include :

- Higher Returns : As the name suggests, these accounts offer a higher annual percentage yield (APY) than standard savings accounts, meaning more money for you over time.
- Liquidity: Unlike some investments, you can access your funds relatively easily, making it suitable for emergency funds or short-term saving goals.
- FDIC Insured: Just like traditional savings accounts, most high-yield savings accounts are insured up to $250,000, offering peace of mind.

The interest rates can change based on economic factors. It's essential to keep an eye on the rates and be prepared for fluctuations. Some accounts might require a minimum balance to earn the high APY or avoid fees.

While high-yield savings accounts offer an enhanced interest rate, investments can provide even more significant potential for returns, albeit with increased risks. The different types of investments include

- **Stocks:** Buying shares of a company. While they can offer high returns, they come with higher risks.
- **Bonds:** Essentially a loan to a company or government, paid back with interest. Generally, they're less risky than stocks but offer lower returns.
- **Mutual Funds:** A pool of funds collected from many investors to buy securities like stocks, bonds, and other assets.
- **Real Estate:** Investing in property, which can provide rental income and potential appreciation in value.

Advantages of Investing

- Potential for High Returns: Historically, investments, especially stocks, have outpaced savings in terms of returns.
- Diversification: Investing allows you to spread your money across various assets, minimizing risks.
- Passive Income : Some investments, like dividend-paying stocks or real estate, can generate regular income.

All investments come with risk. The potential for higher returns often correlates with higher risk. Take into consideration that Some investments, like real estate, aren't easily liquidated, meaning you can't quickly turn them into cash. Successful investing often requires understanding market dynamics, individual assets, and ongoing research. Given the pros and cons of high-yield savings accounts and investments, how do you strike a balance?

High-yield savings are ideal for short-term goals or funds you might need access to soon. Investments are better suited for long-term objectives, like retirement, college savings, or wealth accumulation over decades. If you're risk-averse, you might lean towards high-yield savings. However, if you're open to some risk for potential higher returns, consider diversifying your portfolio with various investments. Your individual goals will dictate your strategy. If you're saving for a down payment on a house in three years, a high-yield savings account is more appropriate. But if you're looking at your financial landscape 30 years down the line, investments become more appealing.

Both high-yield savings accounts and investments have pivotal roles to play. High-yield accounts are the middle ground between traditional savings and investments, offering better returns without exposing you to significant risks. Investments, on the other hand, offer long-term wealth. To navigate these options effectively, arm yourself with knowledge, seek expert advice when needed, and remain adaptable to the ever-changing financial scene.

"Your savings today are the seeds of your dreams tomorrow"

-Anonymous

Savings Sophistication: Elevate Your Money's Potential

Divide your savings into 'buckets' based on goals. For instance, have separate buckets for emergencies, vacations, down payments, or investments. This offers clarity and purpose to every penny saved. With the financial world constantly evolving, new savings instruments and strategies emerge regularly. Stay updated by reading, attending webinars, or consulting with financial advisors.

Initiate monthly or yearly savings challenges. This could be saving every $5 bill you receive or increasing your monthly savings amount by a certain percentage every three months. Sophisticated saving isn't just about what you do right, but also what you avoid.

While it's essential to be cautious, being overly conservative can hinder growth. A well-diversified portfolio often includes a mix of low and moderate-risk instruments. Take account of Inflation. Inflation reduces your money's purchasing power over time. Ensure that at least some of your savings are in instruments that outpace inflation. Elevating your savings game requires a shift in perspective. It's about seeing savings as a dynamic tool to grow wealth.

As you transition from basic saving habits to a more sophisticated approach, remember that every step, decision, and strategy should align with your unique financial goals and vision.

Big Dreams. Bigger Dollars : Mastering Goal-Oriented Saving

Our dreams and aspirations often come with price tags. Goal-oriented savings transform these dreams into realities. Saving for the sake of saving can become tedious. Clear goals provide the motivation and vision to keep going. Without targeted amounts or deadlines, you might not save enough, or you might resort to high-risk investments unnecessarily. Money that's aimlessly saved might miss out on better growth opportunities.

The foundation of goal-oriented saving is the goals themselves. Employ the SMART framework as found in chapter 2.

Clearly define what you're saving for. "Traveling to Italy next summer" is more concrete than "going on a vacation." Attach specific numbers. If that trip to Italy costs $5,000, that's your target. Set goals that are challenging yet attainable, given your income and expenses and ensure your goals align with your broader financial plan and life aspirations. Assign a deadline, knowing you have a year to save for the Italy trip creates urgency and focus.

If you have multiple dreams, rank them. Essential goals like an emergency fund or down payment for a home might take priority over a luxury vacation. For substantial or long-term goals, break them into smaller milestones. Life is dynamic, and so are financial situations. Regularly revisit and adjust your goals as necessary.

For longer-term goals, consider investing a portion of your savings. Generally, the longer the time horizon, the better your portfolio can weather the inherent volatility of stock markets. If investing is new territory, consider consulting a financial advisor. They can guide you based on your goals and risk tolerance. Even with the best-laid plans, setbacks can occur. If you face an unexpected expense, adjust your saving strategy without panicking. Maybe extend the timeline a bit or adjust your monthly savings amount. Dipping into retirement funds or resorting to high-interest loans might seem tempting, but these can harm your long-term financial health. Use setbacks as opportunities to revisit your goals. Ensure they still align with your current situation and aspirations.

Several apps and platforms can aid in goal-oriented saving. Platforms like YNAB or RocketMoney help track expenses, ensuring you remain on target. These tools can determine how much you need to save monthly to achieve your goals within your set time frame. Robo-advisors or investment apps can manage or guide your investments based on your objectives and risk profile.

Bestie, building that financial cushion is the ultimate glow-up. It's not just about security; it's about empowerment. As you nurture and grow your savings, remember, you're not just saving money- you're building a future where you can live your best life, dancing in the rain or sunshine, tossing you all the way from shoestrings to Chanel chains. Your big dreams deserve bigger dollars, and with goal-oriented saving, you're well-equipped to make them come true.

Think of a goal that you've been trying to reach. Every time to reach a saving milestone, fill in the tracker.

Dream Savings Tracker

100% ....

90% ....

80% ....

70% ....

60% ....

50% ....

40% ....

30% ....

20% ....

10% ....

Start: ....

I'm saving for

Why I'm saving for this

Amount

Deadline

Yearly Saving Goals

Use this calendar to map out your yearly savings goals.

JANUARY	FEBRUARY	MARCH
APRIL	MAY	JUNE
JULY	AUGUST	SEPTEMBER
OCOTBER	NOVEMBER	DECEMBER

Chapter Five
Sam is Whose Uncle?

Ah, taxes- the grand stage where the government plays a starring role in your financial performance, but don't worry, I "Gotchu", we'll unravel the mysteries of taxes and make you tax-savvy in no time. I'm all for well-maintained roads, thriving schools, and robust safety nets. There's no need for beef with Uncle Sam; we're here to ensure we make the most of this piece of the financial puzzle.

Meet Emma, a recent college graduate who is filing her taxes for the very first time. As she sits down with her W-2 form and a cup of coffee, Emma begins to navigate the world of tax forms, software, and deductions. However, the unfamiliarity of it all quickly dawns on her. She struggles to decipher the tax jargon and feels overwhelmed by the various sections of the tax return. Emma tries her best, but as she attempts to enter her income, she realizes she's not entirely sure what qualifies as taxable income and what doesn't. Should she include her signing bonus? What about those freelance gigs she took on during the summer?

As she progresses further, she encounters additional hurdles. The software prompts her with complex questions about tax credits, deductions, and dependents. Emma feels like she's trying to solve a puzzle without all the pieces. Despite her initial determination, Emma reaches a point where she's genuinely perplexed by the tax return. Instead of risking costly errors or missed opportunities for deductions, she decides to seek help from a tax professional who can provide guidance tailored to her specific situation.

What that mean?

Unraveling Tax jargon: From AGI to ETC decode the tongue twisters

Tax season can often feel like stepping into a foreign land where a different language is spoken. With terms like AGI, ETC, FICA, W-2, and 1099-INT thrown around, it's no wonder that many people find themselves confused when it comes to taxes.

At the core of the tax language lies AGI, or Adjusted Gross Income. It's the sum of all your income, but it's not as simple as that. We add and subtract various elements to arrive at AGI, which is the starting point for calculating your taxable income. By knowing your AGI, you gain insight into your tax situation, allowing you to plan effectively and optimize your financial strategy.

The choice between itemized and standard deductions can be perplexing. ***Itemized deductions*** involve listing individual expenses such as mortgage interest, medical expenses, and charitable contributions. On the other hand, ***standard deductions*** are fixed amounts you can deduct based on your filing status.

Itemized deductions provide a detailed breakdown of your expenses, allowing you to claim specific deductions that might result in greater tax savings. Conversely, standard deductions offer simplicity and ease, making them a preferred choice for some. Deciding between the two depends on your financial situation. If your itemized deductions surpass the standard deduction amount, itemizing could lead to significant tax savings. However, if your expenses are relatively straightforward, opting for the standard deduction can streamline your tax filing process. It's essential to grasp this concept because your choice directly impacts your taxable income and, consequently, your tax bill.

Tax credits are the secret gems of the tax world. They directly reduce the amount of tax you owe, and some even offer refunds if they exceed your tax liability. Common tax credits include the Child Tax Credit, Earned Income Tax Credit (ETC), and credits for education expenses. Imagine them as financial boosters. They lessen your tax burden and may also provide you with a refund, putting money back into your pocket. The Child Tax Credit, for instance, offers financial relief to parents by reducing their tax liability for each qualifying child. Similarly, the ETC provides substantial assistance to low and moderate-income individuals and families, making it a vital lifeline for many.

Knowing which credits apply to your situation can save you substantial money. In essence, it's like finding hidden treasure in your tax return. By understanding tax credits, you empower yourself to take full advantage of these financial incentives, ensuring you keep more of your hard-earned money.

Tax forms like W-2, 1099-INT, and more are as familiar to tax season as pumpkin spice lattes are to autumn. However, decoding these forms can be a daunting task. Your W-2 form is a crucial piece of your tax puzzle. It's provided by your employer and summarizes your annual earnings, as well as the taxes withheld from your paychecks. It tells you how much you earned and how much has already been allocated to taxes. This information is pivotal when calculating your tax liability.

The 1099-INT form is your gateway to understanding your interest income from bank accounts and investments. The numbers on this form reflect the interest you've earned throughout the year. By comprehending the 1099-INT, you gain insight into the returns generated by your savings and investments.

Form 1040 is where all your tax information comes together. It's the primary form you'll use to file your federal income tax return. This form not only allows you to report your income but also to claim deductions and credits.

From AGI to ETC you can now speak the tax language with confidence. Say goodbye to those tongue twisters, and hello to financial fluency.

The Standard vs. Itemized Deductions Debate

In the world of taxes, one of the biggest debates taxpayers often face is whether to take the standard deduction or itemize their deductions. To make the right choice, it's essential to understand the nuances of both options.

The standard deduction simplifies things. It's a fixed amount that reduces your taxable income, depending on your filing status. In tax year 2023, the standard deduction is:

- Single: $13,850
- Married Filing Jointly: $27,700
- Head of Household: $20,800

Choosing the standard deduction is straightforward, hassle-free, and requires minimal record keeping. If your deductible expenses don't surpass the standard deduction amount, it's often the preferred choice. It provides a significant tax break without the need for extensive documentation. On the flip side, itemized deductions offer a more detailed approach. Instead of claiming a fixed amount, you list specific expenses you've incurred throughout the year, such as:

- Mortgage interest
- Medical expenses
- Charitable contributions
- State and local taxes
- Unreimbursed job-related expenses

Choosing to itemize deductions requires meticulous record-keeping. You'll need to gather receipts, statements, and documents to substantiate your claims. However, the extra effort can be worthwhile if your deductible expenses exceed the standard deduction.

Analyze your financial situation, including your deductible expenses. If your itemized deductions amount to more than the standard deduction for your filing status, itemizing is likely the better choice. Consider your record-keeping habits. Are you diligent about preserving receipts and financial documents? Itemizing requires strict documentation, so ensure you're up for the task. It can be time-consuming so If you have a relatively straightforward tax situation and prefer a quicker filing process, the standard deduction may be more suitable.

You can also opt for using a tax preparation software or hire a tax professional, they can help you determine which option is more advantageous based on your financial details. There's no one-size-fits-all answer. It's a choice that depends on your financial circumstances and preferences. Understanding the fundamentals of both options lets you make an informed decision and optimize your tax strategy. Whether you choose simplicity or detail, the goal is to maximize your tax savings within the boundaries of the law.

"The hardest thing in the world to understand is the income tax."
-Albert Einstein

Did Someone Say TAXmas?

The Tax Trio Forms

Oh Taxmas forms oh taxmas forms – it's the financial event many eagerly anticipate. understanding the key forms and documents involved can turn tax season into a manageable and potentially rewarding experience. Let's dive into the trio of tax essentials: Forms 1040, W-2, and a few more you should know about.

- **Form 1040** is the primary individual income tax return form that U.S. taxpayers use to report their annual income and calculate their tax liability. While there are variations like 1040EZ and 1040A (which have been retired for the tax year 2018 onwards), the classic Form 1040 remains the most versatile. It captures various income sources, including wages, self-employment earnings, interest, dividends, and more. It also allows you to claim deductions, tax credits, and report any taxes you've already paid. Filling out Form 1040 can seem daunting, but it's an essential step in ensuring you meet your tax obligations accurately.

- **Form W-2** is what your employer provides to summarize your annual earnings and the taxes withheld throughout the year. See the following page for a quick breakdown of what you'll find on your W-2.

22222	a Employee's social security number 123-45-6879	OMB No. 1545-0008

b Employer identification number (EIN) 46-1234567	1 Wages, tips, other compensation 55,000.00	2 Federal income tax withheld 4000.00
c Employer's name, address, and ZIP code BESTEST HOSPITAL EVER, INC. 123 PAYNE LANE POSTCALL, NY 11111	3 Social security wages 60,000.00	4 Social security tax withheld 3720.00
	5 Medicare wages and tips 60,000.00	6 Medicare tax withheld 870.00
	7 Social security tips	8 Allocated tips
d Control number	9 Verification code	10 Dependent care benefits
e Employee's first name and initial Last name Suff. DOCTORED B. MONEY 80 WORKHOURS WAY SLEEPLESS HOLLOW, NY 11222	11 Nonqualified plans	12a C 45.50
	13 Statutory employee ☐ Retirement plan ☒ Third-party sick pay ☐	12b E 5000.00
	14 Other NY SDI 31.20	12c DD 9800.57
f Employee's address and ZIP code		12d

15 State	Employer's state ID number	16 State wages, tips, etc.	17 State income tax	18 Local wages, tips, etc.	19 Local income tax	20 Locality name
NY		60,000.00	1500.00	60,000.00	500.00	NYC

Understanding your W-2 is crucial for accurately filing your tax return. It ensures you report the correct income and can claim deductions and credits accurately.

Tax season may also involve additional forms, depending on your financial situation. Some common ones include:

- **Form 1099** Used to report various types of income, such as interest, dividends, and self-employment earnings.
- **Schedule A:** This attachment to Form 1040 allows you to itemize deductions if they exceed the standard deduction.
- **Schedule C**: If you're self-employed or a sole proprietor, this form helps you report your business income and expenses.
- **Schedule D:** Used to report capital gains and losses from investments.
- **Form 8889:** If you have a Health Savings Account (HSA), you'll need this form to report contributions and withdrawals.
- **Form 8862:** If you're claiming the Earned Income Tax Credit (EITC), this form helps ensure you meet the eligibility criteria.

Understanding these forms, when to use them, and how to fill them out correctly can save you time, money, and potential headaches during tax season. Taxmas may never be as exciting as the holidays, but mastering the essentials – like Forms 1040 and W-2 – can make it a lot more manageable. These forms serve as the foundation of your tax return, helping you accurately report your income, deductions, and credits.

Procrastination Prevention: Conquering Your Tax Fears

Let's address the elephant in the room – procrastination. Many people put off filing their taxes until the very last minute, creating unnecessary stress and leaving room for costly mistakes. So why do we procrastinate when it comes to taxes?

The key to conquering your tax fears is proactive tax planning. Instead of waiting until April 15th (or the extended deadline) to scramble through your paperwork, start by gathering all the necessary documents. This includes your W-2, 1099s, receipts for deductible expenses, and any other relevant financial records, which must be distributed to you by 1/31 of each year, as you receive them. Break down the tax preparation process into manageable milestones and Dedicate a specific time each week to tackle one aspect of your taxes, such as gathering receipts or filling out forms.

If your financial situation is complex, don't hesitate to seek the assistance of a tax professional. They can help you navigate the intricacies of tax law and ensure you're taking advantage of all available deductions and credits. Tax laws change, and staying informed about these changes can save you money.

If you're unsure about your tax liability, consult a tax professional who can provide a clearer picture of your financial situation and help you plan accordingly.
By embracing proactive tax planning, staying informed, and addressing the fear of owing money head-on, you can navigate tax season with confidence.

"In this world nothing can be said to be certain, except death and taxes"
-Benjamin Franklin

Dance with deductions: Your Ticket to a refund

Deductions are expenses or contributions that reduce your taxable income. The lower your taxable income, the less you owe in taxes. Earlier in this chapter we spoke about itemized vs standardized deductions, but they can take many more forms.

Above-the-Line Deductions are deductions you can claim before you calculate your adjusted gross income (AGI). They include contributions to retirement accounts and student loan interest payments. Whereas **Below-the-Line Deductions** are subtracted after you've calculated your AGI. They include itemized deductions and the standard deduction.

Now, let's talk about turbocharging your deduction game with tax-advantaged accounts at work. These accounts offer you an opportunity to reduce your taxable income while simultaneously saving for the future.

Contributions to a traditional 401(k) are made with pre-tax dollars, meaning they lower your taxable income for the year. Plus, your investments grow tax-deferred until you withdraw the money in retirement. An FSA allows you to set aside pre-tax dollars for eligible medical and dependent care expenses. It's a smart way to reduce your taxable income and cover essential costs. If you have dependent care expenses, like childcare or eldercare, a DCFSA lets you use pre-tax dollars to cover these costs, lightening your tax load. To make the most of these deductions and tax-advantaged accounts, consider the following:

- Contribute Aggressively: Don't just dip your toes into these accounts; dive in. Max out your contributions to your 401(k), HSA, and FSA to enjoy the maximum tax benefits.

- Itemize Wisely: If you have significant itemized deductions, like mortgage interest or charitable contributions, it might be worth itemizing instead of taking the standard deduction.

- Plan Ahead: Tax planning can happen all year. Routinely evaluate your financial situation and adjust your deductions and contributions accordingly. Twice a year is great for most people, quarterly is better if you run any type of business or work side hustles on top of your job.

- By understanding how deductions work, you can reduce your taxable income and potentially enjoy a refund come tax season. So, don your dancing shoes and embrace the deduction dance.

Making Tax Time Fun

Refund game strong: snatching back those Benjamin

Now, let's talk about the most enjoyable part of tax season: receiving that coveted refund. It's time to make sure your refund game is strong. The path to a robust refund doesn't begin in April; it starts long before that. Throughout the year, consider how you can maximize your deductions and credits to boost your refund. This approach can significantly impact the final amount you receive. Rather than letting your refund quietly slip into your checking account, think about how you can use it strategically. Whether it's paying down high-interest debt, investing in your future, or saving for a significant purchase, your refund can be a powerful tool to help you achieve your financial goals.

Now don't get me wrong, there's no harm in celebrating your refund, but it's crucial to do so responsibly. While it might be tempting to splurge on impulsive purchases, consider using your refund for something meaningful. Let's talk about some tried-and-true strategies to help you secure a more substantial refund.

Unlike deductions that reduce your taxable income, credits directly reduce your tax liability dollar for dollar. Explore available tax credits, such as the Earned Income Tax Credit (EITC), Child Tax Credit, or education-related credits, and ensure you qualify for them.

Adjust your withholding allowances on your W-4 form to align with your financial goals. Claiming fewer allowances results in higher withholding, leading to a potentially larger refund. Keep in mind that this also means you'll have less take-home pay during the year. If you're investing in taxable brokerage accounts, consider tax-efficient mutual funds or exchange-traded funds (ETFs). These investments are designed to minimize taxable distributions, reducing your tax liability. Keep in mind Timing can significantly impact your tax liability. For example, if you're planning a significant charitable donation, make it in the tax year you expect to benefit the most from the deduction. Additionally, timing capital gains or losses can also affect your tax bill.

Something that not a lot of people realize, is that if you or your dependents are pursuing higher education, you can explore education-related tax credits like the American Opportunity Credit or the Lifetime Learning Credit. These credits can help offset education expenses and increase your refund. And don't forget to consider state-specific tax credits. States often offer credits for various activities, such as energy-efficient home improvements or contributions to state-sponsored savings plans.

Remember- getting a larger tax refund isn't about *finessing* the system but rather understanding and utilizing the tax laws to your advantage. By implementing these strategies and staying informed about tax changes, you can maximize your refund and put that extra money toward your financial goals.

Art of Planning: Strategizing for a Stress-Free Tax Season

The thought of sifting through piles of financial documents, deciphering complex tax codes, and worrying about making mistakes can be overwhelming. However, with a strategic approach, you can transform tax season into a stress-free experience. Here's how to plan for a smooth journey through the world of taxes.

Organize Your Documents

The foundation of a stress-free tax season is impeccable organization. Start by creating a dedicated folder or digital repository for all your tax-related documents. This includes W-2s, 1099s, receipts for deductible expenses, and any other income-related documents. Having everything in one place will save you time and frustration.

Stay Updated

Tax laws and regulations change, so it's crucial to stay informed. Follow updates from the IRS and familiarize yourself with any new rules or credits that may affect your tax situation. Being aware of changes in advance can help you prepare more effectively.

Establish a Timeline

Procrastination often leads to stress. Create a timeline for your tax-related tasks, including gathering documents, meeting with a tax professional (if necessary), and filing your return. A well-structured timeline ensures you won't be scrambling at the last minute.

Explore Tax Software
Tax software can simplify the filing process. User-friendly software guides you through each step, checks for errors, and calculates your refund or tax owed. Additionally, many software programs offer e-filing options, which can expedite the processing of your return.

Consider Professional Help
If your financial situation is complex, seeking professional assistance can alleviate stress. A certified tax professional can navigate intricate tax laws, identify deductions you might miss, and ensure your return is accurate.

Keep Meticulous Records
Accurate record-keeping is essential. Maintain a detailed record of all income and expenses, including receipts and invoices. If you're audited or have questions about your return, having organized records can be a lifesaver.

Stay calm and Ask for Help
If you encounter challenges or uncertainties during tax season, don't hesitate to seek assistance. Asking for help from a tax professional, or even knowledgeable family /friends can provide clarity and peace of mind.

Tax season doesn't have to be synonymous with stress. You can navigate the tax landscape confidently, ensuring a successful tax season.

"A person doesn't know how much he has to be thankful for until he has to pay taxes on it."
-Anonymous

Tax survival kit: Bite sized Tax wisdom

- Just like you update your playlist, regularly review your W-4 to make sure you're not overpaying or leaving money on the table.

- E-filing is the modern way to do taxes. It's like ordering your favorite meal online—fast and error-free...Most of the time

- Stay informed about tax changes, especially after major life events. It's like leveling up in this game of life.

- Your state taxes are like the side quests in the tax game. Don't forget to complete them for a potentially bigger refund.

- Procrastination? Nope! Start early, review often, and you'll finish your taxes on time and with a smile. When in doubt, seek a tax pro's help. It's like having your own personal guide.

- Think of saving for taxes like saving for a concert ticket. When it's showtime, you've got a front-row seat!

- Charity receipts are your golden tickets to tax deductions. Keep them organized, like you do with your favorite collectibles.

- Accuracy is key! Double-check your tax return, just like you double-check that risky text.

- Hold on to past tax return transcripts. They may come in handy someday.

- Plan for next year's taxes. It's like setting resolutions for your financial well-being. Watch out for tax scams. Guard your personal info.

The good news? taxes are just another dance. and you've got moves better than Usher!

The Deduction Circle (page 1)

Use this list to identify potential deductions and credits you may qualify for, but may not have been aware of. Fill in each slice on the following page if you qualify for any of the deductions or credits below.

Potential Deductions

- Home mortgage interest (Form 1098).
- Real estate and personal property taxes paid.
- State and local income taxes or sales taxes paid.
- Medical and dental expenses.
- Charitable contributions.
- Education expenses (tuition, fees, student loan interest).
- Retirement contributions (e.g., IRA, 401(k)).
- Job-related expenses (for employees and self-employed).
- Child care costs.

Potential Credits

- Education credits (e.g., American Opportunity Credit).
- Child Tax Credit.
- Earned Income Tax Credit (EITC).
- Energy-efficient home improvements.
- Elderly or Disabled Credit.

The Deduction Circle (page 2)

Use the list on the previous page to help you identify potential deductions and credits. Fill in each slice on this page if you qualify for any of the deductions or credits mentioned.

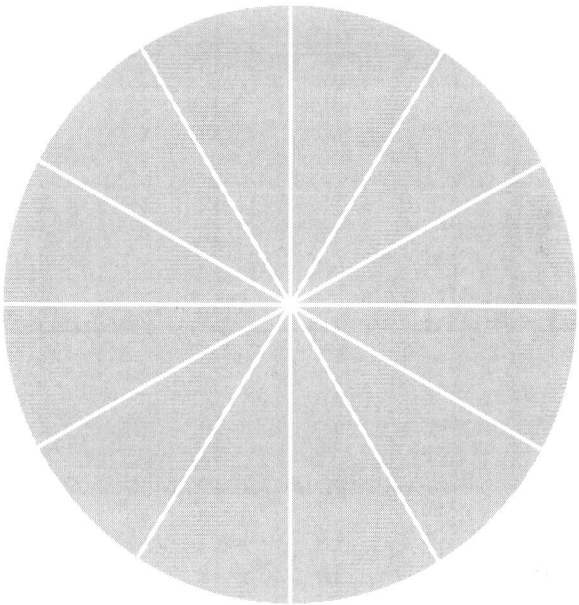

NOTES

Chapter Six
Money Making Money

One of the easiest ways I've increased my net worth is contributing to retirement accounts with my employer. Let's do some math, let's say that you were able to get your budget and income to the place where you can contribute the IRS allowed maximum to the company's retirement plan for the next 10 years. The maximum changes each year but is traditionally around the $20,000 mark.

If your company also matches 5%, that means you're putting away more than $200,000 over 10 years. Do you have a better way to put away $200,000 for yourself? If you do, please share! In this chapter We'll talk about getting your money to make money for you by putting it in the right places.

"Invest in yourself. You can afford it. Trust me."

– Rashon Carraway

The easiest way to invest your 401K/403B and Roth IRA

Your employer's matching contribution is essentially free money. Let's break it down. Imagine your employer offers a 100% match on your contributions up to 3% of your salary. If you earn $50,000 a year and contribute 3% ($1,500), your employer chips in an additional $1,500. That's an instant 100% return on your investment. It's like doubling your money without even trying. So, always contribute enough to max out the match – it's the smartest move in your retirement playbook.

We get it; life is busy. It's easy to forget to invest regularly. That's why automatic contributions are your secret weapon. When you set up automatic deductions from your paycheck to your 401(k) or 403(b), You won't even miss the money, but future you is thanking the current you in the mirror. Your 401(k) or 403(b) likely offers a range of investment options, from stocks to bonds and everything in between. By diversifying, you're reducing risk and increasing the odds of a healthy return.

Now, let's talk Roth IRA. With a Roth IRA, you're contributing after-tax dollars, meaning you've already paid Uncle Sam his cut. But here's the kicker: when you retire and start withdrawing your money, it's all tax-free. No capital gains taxes, no income taxes – it's a sweet deal. If you haven't opened one yet, consider this your financial wake-up call. Each year, the IRS sets a maximum contribution limit for Roth IRAs. For 2023, it's $6,000 (or $7,000 if you're 50 or older). The trick is to try and max it out if you can swing it. Why? Because that's more money growing tax-free for your retirement dreams. Plus, if you start early, those contributions can compound into a substantial nest egg.

Investment fees can quietly nibble away at your returns. Opt for low-cost index funds or exchange-traded funds (ETFs). They offer diversified portfolios at a fraction of the cost of actively managed funds. They're just as good but way cheaper. Periodically review your investment choices. As you age and get closer to retirement, you might want to shift your portfolio to be a bit less aggressive. Your risk tolerance and goals can change, so don't hesitate to make adjustments accordingly.

If you're wondering when you should make changes, a good guideline is a few months after you have a significant life event such as a move, marriage or divorce, birth or death of an immediate family member. If your life doesn't change that much, then look at it every 3 or 5 years, you might be pleasantly surprised at how good your future accounts look.

A cautionary tale: don't raid your retirement accounts unless it's an emergency. The power of compound interest works best when you let your investments grow over time. When you withdraw early, you not only lose out on potential growth but might face penalties and taxes. If all this talk about stocks, bonds, and IRAs makes your head spin, consider consulting a financial advisor. A good advisor can help you craft a personalized investment strategy that aligns with your goals and risk tolerance. Not sure where to find one? Your employer likely offers basic retirement advice through the retirement administrator. If you decide to hire someone on your own, look for someone who is fee based and is a fiduciary, this means they must put your best interest ahead of their own. Remember, investing is a long game. Be patient, stay diversified, and let time do its magic.

Your future self will be sipping cocktails on a beach somewhere, thanking you for these savvy money moves.

Investments: Risk and Reward

When it comes to investing, there is some risk involved. When you buy a stock, you're purchasing a share of ownership in a company. You are a shareholder, which means you have a say in the company's decisions, and you share in its profits and or losses. Stocks can be a powerful wealth-building tool, but they come with risks. Prices can be volatile, and it's important to research companies before investing.

What about bonds? Think of bonds as loans you provide to governments or companies. In return, they promise to pay you back the principal amount, along with periodic interest payments. Bonds are generally considered lower risk compared to stocks, making them a more conservative investment option. They're like the stability in your investment portfolio.

Diversification is a fundamental strategy in investing. It means spreading your investments across various asset classes like stocks, bonds, and possibly real estate or commodities. Diversifying helps reduce risk because if one asset class underperforms, others may compensate. It's how you avoid putting all your eggs in one basket. Mutual funds and ETFs offer a convenient way to diversify your investments without picking individual stocks or bonds. A mutual fund pools money from many investors to buy a diversified portfolio of stocks, bonds, or other securities. ETFs are similar but are traded on stock exchanges like individual stocks. These options provide instant diversification without the need for extensive research.

"And I'mma say this in the most humblest way possible, I'm a millionaire"

-Cardi B

Investing in real estate involves purchasing properties or real estate investment trusts (REITs). It can be a source of rental income and potential appreciation in property values. However, real estate investments can be hands-on, requiring management and maintenance.

Your risk tolerance refers to how comfortable you are with the possibility of losing money on your investments. Your investment horizon is the time you plan to hold your investments before needing the money. These factors influence your choice of investments. If you have a longer horizon and higher risk tolerance, you may lean more towards stocks. We've stripped away the complexity and focused on the essentials of investing. It's about understanding the various investment options available and aligning them with your financial goals and comfort level. Remember, investing is a journey, and finesse comes with knowledge and experience.

Decoding Investment Jargon: From Bulls & Bears To Dividends & Yield

Let's decode the financial lingo that might sound like gibberish. By the end of this chapter, you'll speak investment fluently, from bulls and bears to dividends and yield. In the world of investing, you'll frequently hear about *"**bull markets**"* and *"**bear markets.**"* But what do these terms mean? A bull market is like a charging bull – it represents a period of rising stock prices and optimism about the market's future. On the flip side, a bear market is like a hibernating bear – it signifies a market downturn with falling stock prices and pessimism.

Let's look at some other investment lingo that you should know if you want to talk the talk.

- **Dividends**

Dividends are your share of a company's profits. When a company makes money, it can choose to distribute a portion of those earnings to its shareholders as dividends. Think of dividends as your slice of the profit pie. They can provide a steady stream of income in addition to potential stock price appreciation.

- **Yield**

Yield is a term often associated with bonds. It represents the income you earn from a bond, typically expressed as a percentage of the bond's face value. Yield takes into account the bond's interest payments and its current market price. Understanding yield helps you assess the income potential of bond investments.

- **Market Volatility**

Volatility refers to the rapid and significant price fluctuations in the market. It's like the ups and downs of the investment market. Market volatility can impact the value of your investments. Being prepared for market swings is key to maintaining your financial composure. There is a real-time market index representing the market's expectations for volatility in the S&P 5 over the coming 30 days. VIX, no, not the stuff your abuela cures you with, VIX is the Chicago Board Options Exchange's (CBOE) Volatility Index.

- **Risk Tolerance and Risk Assessment**

Your risk tolerance is your ability and willingness to withstand investment losses. It's influenced by your financial goals, time horizon, and temperament, all of which are heavily shaped by your formative experiences with money as a young adult (go back to Chapter 1). To make informed investment decisions, you'll need to assess your risk tolerance accurately. It's like knowing your comfort level– some love the thrill, while others prefer a gentler ride.

- **Asset Allocation**

Asset allocation involves dividing your investments among different asset classes based on your financial goals and risk tolerance. By diversifying your investments, you aim to achieve the right mix of assets to meet your objectives. Asset anything of value owned by an individual or corporation.

- **Bond**

A debt security that pays periodic interest and returns the principal at maturity.

- **Capital Gain**

Profit from the sale of a security or real estate.

- **Equity**

Ownership interest in a company, typically in the form of stock.

- **ETF (Exchange Traded Fund**)

An investment fund traded on stock exchanges, typically holding assets like stocks, bonds, or commodities.

- **Hedge**

An investment made to reduce or offset the potential loss or risk from another investment. Essentially, hedging is a form of risk management. Imagine you have invested in a particular asset that might lose value under certain circumstances. To protect yourself from potential losses, you might make another investment (the hedge) that will gain value under those same circumstances.

- **IPO (Initial Public Offering)**

The first sale of stock by a private company to the public.

- **Liquidity**

The ease with which an asset can be converted into cash.

- **Mutual Fund**

An investment vehicle that pools together money from many people to purchase a diversified portfolio of stocks, bonds, or other securities.

- **Portfolio**

A collection of investments owned by an individual or institution.

- **REIT (Real Estate Investment Trust)**

A company that owns, operates, or finances income-producing real estate.

- **ROI (Return on Investment)**

A measure used to evaluate the profitability of an investment.

- **Short Selling**

Short selling is a trading strategy where an investor borrows shares of a stock and sells them, anticipating a price decline. The goal is to later buy the shares back at a lower price, return the borrowed shares, and pocket the difference as profit. If the stock price rises, or if the broker needs the borrowed shares back, an investor might be forced to buy back at an unfavorable price

- **Blue Chip Stocks**

Stocks of well-established companies known for their stability and performance.

- **Margin Call**

A broker's demand for additional funds due to declining asset values in a margin account.

- **P/E Ratio (Price-to-Earnings Ratio)**

A valuation ratio calculated by dividing the market price of a stock by its earnings per share.

- **Capital Allocation**

The process of distributing financial resources to different assets.

Crafting a Diversified Ensemble Of Investments

Diversification is how you manage risk spreading your investments across different asset classes. This diversification helps cushion your portfolio against the ups and downs of individual investments. To create a diversified investment portfolio, decide how much of your portfolio will be in each asset class. This allocation depends on factors like your financial goals, risk tolerance, and time horizon - this is the amount of time you expect to pass before you want to use the money tied up in investments.

Once you've determined your asset allocation, choose specific investments within each class. For example, if you decide to invest in stocks, consider the different types. Assess your risk tolerance honestly. If you can't sleep at night when your investments are down, you may need a more conservative allocation. Over time, your portfolio's performance may cause it to drift from your desired allocation. Periodically rebalance by buying or selling assets to bring it back in line.

Why Diversify?

Diversification aims to reduce risk. When one asset class underperforms, others may do well, offsetting losses. It's not about trying to predict which investments will perform best but rather about managing risk. Crafting a diversified investment portfolio can be complex, and professional advice can be invaluable. Your portfolio should be tailored to your unique financial situation and objectives. Building a diversified investment portfolio might not sound flashy, but it's a solid strategy that can lead to financial stability and growth.

Want an easy button? Index funds and EFTs do this for you, go back to the beginning of this chapter to remind yourself what those are.

You want your investments to match your energy on risk.

Here's the deal: if you want higher potential rewards, you typically have to take on more risk. But, that doesn't mean you should throw caution to the wind and bet the farm on a single high-risk investment. Before we dive deeper, let's figure out your risk tolerance. Think about it this way; If wild price swings make you queasy, you might lean towards a more conservative approach. So, which one are ya?

- **Low Risk Tolerance:** You prefer stability and are willing to accept lower returns to avoid significant losses.

- **Moderate Risk Tolerance:** You're okay with a little turbulence in exchange for potential higher returns.

- **High Risk Tolerance:** You've got nerves of steel and are ready to embrace volatility for the chance of substantial gains.

Once you've gauged your risk tolerance, it's time to align your investments accordingly. Here's a straightforward breakdown:

Those with low risk tolerance should focus on investments with lower volatility, like bonds and stable dividend- paying stocks. These provide regular income and have historically been less prone to wild price swings.

Folks with moderate risk tolerance are in the middle of the road, so consider a mix of stocks and bonds. This provides potential for growth while cushioning against major losses. Diversification is your BFF.

If you have high risk tolerance go ahead and explore higher-risk investments like growth stocks or even venture into the world of cryptocurrencies. Just remember that with greater potential rewards come greater potential losses.

Your risk tolerance can change over time. Life events, market experiences, and personal circumstances all play a role. Periodically review your investment strategy and make adjustments to ensure it still matches your comfort level and goals. embrace the balance of risk and reward that suits you best and keep moving forward.

Investing with Intention: Aligning Your Portfolio With Your Financial Goals

It's time to get practical and dive deep into aligning your investment portfolio with your financial goals. Before you even think about investments, take a moment to reflect on your financial goals. What do you want to achieve? Be specific. Whether it's buying a home, launching a business, or retiring early to travel the world, clarity is king.

The Goals, They Are A-Changin'

Different goals have different timelines. Some are short-term, like a dream vacation in a year, while others, like retirement, are long-term. Life isn't static, and neither are your goals. Flexibility is your friend. Life rarely goes according to plan, so be prepared to adjust your portfolio when necessary. Unexpected expenses or windfalls may require you to pivot your investment strategy. Knowing the time horizon of each goal will help you determine the appropriate level of risk for each investment. Take into account your financial situation, age, and psychological comfort with investment volatility. This will influence the asset allocation suitable for each goal.

- **Short-Term Goals:** Consider more conservative investments like money market funds, CDs, or short- term bonds.
- **Medium-Term Goals:** Balanced funds, bond ladders, or certain less-volatile stocks might be suitable.
- **Long-Term Goals:** Stocks, mutual funds, ETFs, or real estate can be considered due to their potential for higher returns over longer periods.

Set an asset allocation for each goal. Distribute your investments among stocks, bonds, and other assets. For riskier, long-term goals, a higher percentage might be in stocks, while for short-term goals, you might favor bonds or cash equivalents. Next, calculate how much to invest.

Based on the expected rate of return and the time horizon combined, determine how much you need to invest regularly to achieve each goal. As you approach each goal's time horizon, consider shifting to more conservative investments to protect gains. Rebalance your portfolio if certain assets deviate from your desired allocation due to market movements. It's essential to stay informed about your. investments, but information overload can lead to analysis paralysis. Find a balance between keeping an eye on your portfolio and getting overwhelmed by every market twist and turn.

Remember that investing is a long-term game. Impatience can lead to hasty decisions and unnecessary losses. Stick to your strategy, stay focused on your goals, and let time do its magic.

"Do not save what is left after spending, but spend what is left after saving."

-Warren Buffett

Early Retirement Anyone?

Retirement Realness: Planning For The Golden Years

Retirement might seem distant, but the best time to plan for those golden years is now. Time is money, especially when compound interest is involved. Begin with a clear picture of when you want to retire. Whether it's the standard 65 or an ambitious 50, your retirement age sets the stage for your planning. To estimate your retirement expenses, think about housing, healthcare, daily living costs, and any other financial obligations you might have for children, parents or businesses. Be realistic about your lifestyle expectations. Something to also consider, is how long the people in your family live? Do you have health conditions or life's circumstances that might push you to retire earlier than 65? Do you think you'll be one of 32%of Americans over the age 65 who still work?

If your employer offers a retirement plan like a 401(k), participate. At the very least, make sure you contribute enough to get any employer match –easiest money you might ever make. As you're planning for decades of retirement, your investment strategy should focus on long-term growth. Consider opening an IRA. Traditional IRAs offer tax-deferred growth, while Roth IRAs provide tax-free withdrawals in retirement. Choose the one that aligns with your tax strategy. Keep in mind that High fees can eat into your retirement savings. Choose low-cost investment options, like index funds or ETFs, to maximize your returns.

Build an emergency fund for unexpected expenses, too. It's painfully easy to underestimate the healthcare costs in retirement, especially if it's more than 10 years away. When the time comes, be sure to investigate Medicare options and consider supplementing insurance policies to cover potential gaps. For right now, take the time to regularly review your retirement plan. This doesn't have to be a big to-do, it could be a once a year check, perhaps in the fall when you're signing up for benefits at your job, to confirm you contribution and investments are where you want them to stay on track. Don't forget to prepare a will and consider creating a trust if your finances and/or family situation is complex.

Estate planning helps to make sure your assets go where you want them to after you're gone, and can help to reduce the taxes and fees your surviving loved ones have to pay to use what you've left for them. If you're employed and your job offers retirement or life insurance benefits, you probably have access to free or very low cost help with preparing a will through the life-insurance administrator or employee assistance program (EAP).

Planning for retirement is a serious endeavor, but it doesn't need to be daunting. By following these straightforward steps and staying focused on your financial future, you'll be better prepared to enjoy your golden years with financial security and peace of mind.

Crafting A Life Of Leisure On Your Terms

Retirement planning goes beyond financial security; it's about achieving your desired lifestyle on your own terms. a well-structured budget remains your trusted ally. Plan for both essential expenses and leisure activities to ensure your finances support your desired lifestyle. Prudent spending habits can help your savings last longer. Track your expenses and make informed decisions about your discretionary spending.

Stay socially active during retirement. Join clubs, attend events, or volunteer. Social connections are essential for emotional well-being. Continue learning and challenging your mind. Pursue intellectual interests or engage in activities that promote cognitive health. Maintain an active and healthy lifestyle. Regular exercise and a balanced diet contribute to your overall well-being.

If you have specific wishes for your legacy, such as funding education for grandchildren or supporting a charitable foundation, outline these intentions clearly in your estate plan. Crafting a financially secure retirement involves more than just saving money; it requires strategic planning and thoughtful decision-making, so you can achieve the lifestyle you desire while safeguarding your financial well- being.

Planning the Legacy You Leave Behind

Estate planning is not only for rich people, regular people need to do it too! If you own and/or owe anything, having an estate plan gives you power to control where your money and things go when you become somebody's ancestor. How do you do it? Begin by reflecting on your core values and what matters most to you. Understanding your values will guide your decisions on where and how to leave a legacy. Consider the financial well-being and relationship dynamics of your family.

Pro Tip

Talk to an attorney who can help you write a will or start a trust. If you are employed, you may have access to free or discounted legal services through your employer. Check with your HR/Benefits department to see the company offers an Employee Assistance Program (EAP) or if it's available as a service through the company that provides the life insurance coverage that's part of your benefits.

A well-crafted estate plan is crucial for ensuring your assets are distributed according to your wishes. Work with professionals to create a comprehensive plan that minimizes taxes and legal complications. If you own a business, plan for its future beyond your involvement. Succession planning ensures a smooth transition. Whether you pass it on to family members or sell it.

Your legacy is an enduring testament to the values and principles you hold dear. By planning with purpose, you can create a legacy that positively influences future generations and leaves the world a better place. Whether you seek to support your family, charitable causes, or both, thoughtful planning can ensure your legacy reflects the values and principles that matter most to you.

Investment Dreamboard

Jot down your investment goals using this investment dreamboard. Color in the first column once you've invested in the corresponding company.

INVESTED?	TYPE/NAME	COST	AMOUNT	DATE
		TOTAL		

Chapter Seven
It's Giving...Generous

As we delve into this chapter, we'll unveil the transformative potential of intentional giving. From helping your family, to strategically choosing causes that align with your values, we'll explore how generosity can elevate not only the lives of others but also your own financial well-being.

On My Mama: Putting Family In The Budget

When I was finishing my master's degree, I was laser focused on graduating with three things, a car, a professional job with benefits, and money in my savings account in case I needed to move for the job. My second year in the public health program I was working three or four jobs so that I could meet my goals. My younger sister, Nina, was also on campus with me as an undergraduate student and our younger brother was a high school student back home in a Detroit suburb with our mom.

At that time in my life it was really deeply important to me to help my family because I always felt like I didn't have a safety net, but I could be that for my siblings especially. This usually came in the form of small things like football cleats, money toward a homecoming dress, or the occasional bill. About 3 months before graduation, my mom called and asked me for money, something reasonable like $100 to cover an unexpected bill. On the phone I took a deep breath and told my mom that I would send the money, but under one condition. I heard her get quiet on the other end of the line, kinda like she was waiting for me to give her a hard time about her request. I told her, "Mom, you know I'm really working hard on my budget, right?" She said, "yes, I do, how many jobs are you working at today? Just two or all three?"

I went on to tell her that I looked at my bank statements and notice that I was sending her the equivalent of about $150 a month, and as she started to share the reasons, I interrupted her (dangerous when you have a mama like mine, even from 50 miles away) and said, I have no problem sending it but you keep throwing off my budget because you're not always asking for the same amount or when you need it moves around and isn't always when I have cash in the right account. She tentatively said OK. And I went on to ask her if she had a bill that was $175 or $200 that I could take over. Because "I like helping, I'm glad to actually, I just need to do it in a way that works in my budget and around my paychecks." She thought for a moment and said, "yeah, my car insurance is $177." I replied, "ok, here's what I would like to do, tell me what day of the month it's due and send me a copy of the bill so I can pay it every month. Starting next month, it's my bill now. Maybe that will give you enough wiggle room in your budget so you won't have to call me."

And it worked! I didn't get calls for money for years after we made this arrangement. This allowed me to free up room in her budget in a way that worked for mine.

Having a desire to make a positive impact on your family and in the world doesn't have to be in conflict with your overall financial goals. It just takes some creativity about how to support causes close to your heart, on your budget. Balancing your generous intentions with the financial realities of your life is possible.

The Art of Giving

Guiding Your Heart: Merging Financial Prudence With Acts Of Kindness

Giving, whether through financial contributions or acts of kindness, has the power to transform not only the lives of those you help but your own life as well. Generosity is often born from a heartfelt desire to make a positive impact on the world around us. It's an intrinsic part of our humanity, allowing us to connect with others and create a sense of belonging in our communities. Many of us aspire to give back to society, whether by supporting a local charity, helping those in need, or contributing to causes that resonate with our values. The desire to give must be harmoniously balanced with sound financial planning. We understand that each person's financial situation is unique, and it's crucial to give within your means. The goal is to ensure that your philanthropic efforts enhance your financial well-being instead of hindering it.

One of the key concepts you need is how to establish a giving budget. Similar to a personal financial budget, a giving budget outlines how much you can allocate for charitable contributions without compromising your financial goals. considering your income, expenses, and financial objectives. Before contributing, it's essential to research and evaluate charitable organizations. Maximizing the impact of your giving involves utilizing tax-efficient strategies. you can leverage tax incentives and deductions to make your donations go further.

This includes charitable deductions, donor-advised funds, and other tax-efficient giving options. You can typically deduct charitable contributions up to 60% of your adjusted gross income (AGI), though there are some nuances based on the type of contribution and the organization.

Donor-Advised Funds (DAFs) are accounts dedicated to charitable giving. You contribute to the fund, receive an immediate tax deduction, and then recommend grants from the fund to your chosen charities over time. Contributions to DAFs are deductible in the year they are made. This can be especially beneficial in a high-income year to offset a larger tax liability. While you get the tax deduction immediately, you can take your time deciding which charities to support, allowing for thoughtful philanthropy.

Charitable Remainder Trusts (CRTs) Transfer appreciated assets into a trust. The trust then sells the assets and provides you with an income stream. Some benefits of this include avoiding immediate capital gains tax, receiving an income, and getting a tax deduction for the charitable portion of the trust.

Qualified Charitable Distributions (QCDs). If you're over 70½ and have an IRA, you can directly transfer up to $100,000 annually from the IRA to a qualified charity. The distribution isn't included in your taxable income and counts toward your required minimum distribution.

Charitable Lead Trusts (CLTs) Assets are placed in a trust that pays a fixed amount to a charity for a specified period. At the end of the period, the remaining assets go to beneficiaries, often at reduced or eliminated gift or estate tax.

Tax laws change, and not all charities qualify for tax-deductible contributions. Regularly consult with tax professionals and financial advisors to ensure your giving is both impactful and tax-efficient. Leveraging these strategies not only maximizes the impact of your giving but can also align your financial planning with philanthropic goals.

For those who wish to contribute in different ways, creative methods of giving includes volunteering, donating goods, services, or expertise to organizations or individuals in need. In-kind contributions can be just as valuable as monetary donations and allow you to provide support within your means. Giving should be a thoughtful and intentional act, driven by your values and desire to make a difference. Identify the causes and organizations that resonate with you personally.

Honoring Your Values Through Giving

Let's talk about the significance of aligning your charitable giving with your core values. It's important to understand that each individual's values are unique, and your philanthropic efforts should reflect what truly matters to you and not what the next celebrity is doing.

Before delving into charitable giving, it's essential to identify your core values. These values shape your beliefs, behaviors, and priorities. Pinpointing your core values for giving is a deeply introspective process. It ensures your charitable endeavors resonate with what you genuinely care about.

First, reflect on your personal experiences. Think about moments when you felt most content, fulfilled, or passionate. What caused these feelings? Conversely, consider times you felt dismayed or frustrated—often, these emotions arise when our values are compromised. On a piece of paper, jot down words that resonate with you: compassion, justice, sustainability, education, health, etc. This list doesn't have to be perfect; it's just a starting point. Now Imagine you have a significant sum of money to donate. Think about where you'd want that money to go and the impact you'd like to see based on the list you just made. This can give insights into what truly matters to you.

Next, reflect on your previous donations or volunteer activities. Are there recurring themes or causes you gravitate towards? What injustices in the world do you feel most strongly about? When you watch the news, which stories evoke the strongest reactions from you? Now, from your brainstormed list, select the top three or five values most significant to you. It's essential to narrow down to ensure focus. Once you've pinpointed your core values for giving, you can seek out charities, organizations, or initiatives that align with these values, ensuring your contributions are both impactful and personally meaningful. As you grow and evolve, so might your values. Revisit them periodically to ensure they still align with your beliefs and feelings.

Giving with purpose enhances the satisfaction derived from your contributions. We emphasize the idea that giving isn't solely about monetary donations. Volunteering your time, skills, or expertise can be equally impactful. Whether you're passionate about education, healthcare, or environmental conservation, be empowered to make a difference that resonates with your heart and soul.

Balancing Charitable Intentions With Financial Realities

Before you start giving, you'll need to set clear, achievable giving goals that are feasible within your financial capacity. Whether you're a recent college graduate just starting your career or someone looking to increase their charitable contributions, it's important to set realistic goals. Incorporating charitable giving into your budget is essential. While giving is important, maintaining your own financial well-being must take precedence. Let me once again stress the importance of covering your essential needs, building an emergency fund, and managing debt before allocating funds for charitable giving. Financial stability enables you to give more effectively and sustainably.

As your financial situation evolves, your giving can grow too. Incrementally increasing your charitable contributions in tandem with your income growth is a strategic way to ensure your philanthropic efforts scale with your financial capacity. Decide on a fixed percentage of your income that you're comfortable donating. For instance, if you currently give 3% of your income, maintain that percentage as your income grows. As time goes on, consider gradually increasing the percentage. For example, for every 10% increase in income, you might raise your giving by 0.5%. At the end of each year, review your income growth. If you've received a raise, bonus, or additional income, calculate the increased amount you can donate based on your decided percentage.

However, if new financial obligations arise, such as a mortgage or tuition, factor them into your calculations.
As your contributions grow, consider diversifying how you give. Explore options like donor-advised funds, charitable trusts, or endowments, which can be more tax-efficient and impactful in the long run. As your career progresses and income potentially grows, set charitable milestones. For example, "when my income reaches X, I aim to donate Y amount or Z%." If you consistently meet your given milestones, challenge yourself by setting new, higher benchmarks.

Many employers offer donation match programs. As you increase your contributions, ensure you're maximizing any available matching programs. By aligning charitable contributions with income growth, you ensure that you're giving scales sustainably, allowing you to make a more significant impact over time without compromising your financial well- being. Life can be unpredictable, and financial challenges may arise. Regularly assessing your giving plan is essential.

I encourage everyone to give with a compassionate heart while also prioritizing their financial health. Finding this equilibrium allows you to make a positive impact on the causes you care about while securing your own financial well-being.

Skillful Giving

"Those who are happiest are those
who do the most for others"

-Booker T. Washington

Sharing Your Expertise to Empower Others

In an era where knowledge is power, skillful giving stands out as a profound way to make a difference. It goes beyond monetary donations, focusing on sharing expertise, skills, and knowledge to empower individuals, organizations, and communities. Let's explore the dynamics of this unique form of philanthropy

Skillful giving revolves around contributing one's specialized skills or knowledge for the betterment of others, often pro bono. Whether you're a graphic designer, educator, financial expert, or craftsman, there's a world out there that can benefit from your expertise. Teaching and sharing refine your skills and expand your perspective. By imparting skills, you enable others to be self-reliant, creating a lasting impact. Expertise can help nonprofits or underserved communities access services they might not otherwise afford. Offer your services to NGOs, schools, or community centers.

Platforms like Catchafire or Taproot can connect professionals with organizations in need OR use platforms like Coursera, Udemy, or YouTube to create courses or tutorials. You can also organize free sessions on your area of expertise, a financial consultant might host a basic financial literacy workshop for underprivileged youth etc. Start local, Understand the needs of your community or the challenges faced by nearby organizations.

Giving can be time-consuming. Set clear boundaries and decide in advance the time you can allocate. Be clear about the scope of your contribution to ensure organizations or individuals have realistic expectations. There's a unique satisfaction in seeing someone flourish using the knowledge you've imparted. When working with diverse communities, it's essential to approach with respect and understanding. This often leads to meaningful relationships and networks. It can enhance your professional reputation, showcasing not only your expertise but also your commitment to social responsibility. As you give back, you also learn. Stay updated in your field to ensure you're providing current and relevant expertise.

By sharing expertise, you not only uplift others but also enrich your journey, proving that sometimes, the most valuable gift one can offer is knowledge.

Light Of Positivity: Your Impact Through Volunteerism

Volunteerism illuminates the world with the glow of positivity, proving that actions, often more than words or money, have the power to bring about transformative change. At its core, volunteerism is the selfless act of dedicating one's time and energy to benefit others without expecting monetary rewards. It's a testament to the human spirit's capacity for empathy and compassion. Your actions can lead to immediate change, such as building homes, teaching, or providing medical care. The ripple effect of volunteerism can inspire others to take action or uplift the spirits of an entire community.

Ensure that your contributions are sustainable. For example, training local communities ensures that they can carry on the initiatives even after you've completed your volunteering stint. It's essential to balance volunteering with personal and professional responsibilities. Share your experiences through blogs, social media, or conversations. Your stories can inspire others to embark on their volunteer journeys. Stay connected with the communities or organizations you've volunteered in.

Regular updates can keep you informed and offer opportunities for further involvement. Beyond the tangible impacts, recognize the intangible rewards: the smiles you bring, the hope you instill, and the love you share.

Weaving Financial Wisdom Into Your Acts Of Generosity

Generosity, in all its forms, has the power to touch lives. Understand that while the intent is paramount, the means matter. Donating beyond one's capacity might feel heroic initially but can lead to personal financial stress.

Are you looking to provide immediate relief, like disaster aid, or invest in long-term community development? Decide whether you want your contributions to benefit local communities or address global challenges. If cash donations aren't feasible, consider other forms of generosity. Volunteering like we looked at above, mentoring, or providing pro-bono services can be incredibly valuable. Instead of a single large donation, consider spreading your contributions across various causes or stagger them over time. This approach mirrors the diversification strategy in investments. Ensure you have an emergency fund or savings buffer. crucial to be prepared for unforeseen personal financial needs.

Just as you'd review an investment portfolio, periodically assess your charitable contributions to ensure they align with your evolving financial situation and philanthropic goals. Pooling resources with friends, family, or community members can amplify the impact. Collective efforts can fund larger projects or support multiple causes. Weaving financial wisdom into acts of generosity ensures that your philanthropic journey is not only heartfelt but also sustainable and impactful. Generosity is a beautiful expression of your compassion. Let’s strive to cultivate a legacy of kindness and make a positive imprint on the world around us, one heartfelt act at a time.

“Life's most persistent and urgent question is what are you doing for others?”

-Martin Luther King Jr

Donation Tracker

Use this activity sheet to track your donations for the month. Put an "X" through each day you donated or participated in anything philanthropic

1	2	3	4	5	6	7	8
9	10	11	12	13	14	15	16
17	18	19	20	21	22	23	24
25	26	27	28	29	30	31	

NOTES

Chapter Eight

Minding The Business That Pays You

Jobs are how most people make the money that funds their life. Are you in the driver's seat of your career? What is guiding you along the way? Stars? GPS? Directions from well-meaning friends and relatives who've been there? Let's find out! Are you working on building your career or are you still slogging your way to a job every day? We're talking about careers because if you're reading this book, you are probably not independently wealthy yet, and have to trade your time, talents, and skills for money. Let's make sure you're getting the most money when you do.

"Climbing the ladder? Honey, I'm taking the elevator."

-Anonymous

Fusing Dreams With Dollars: Paving Your Way To Fiscal Triumph

When you are starting a job search, you might think the first step is to update your resume. Wrong! You actually need to check your budget. If you don't deeply understand what it cost you to live, and whether you have any new or increased expenses coming up, you are almost guaranteed to leave money on the table.

Once you've checked and recalibrated your magic number, you can move on to evaluating potential employers. You'll want to get any information you can on growth opportunities, the company culture, and how a potential job change aligns with your long-term career objectives. Weighing the potential increase in salary, better benefits, and improved work-life balance against the risks and the unknowns is part of this pivotal decision- making process. It's also prudent to consider the stability and reputation of the prospective employer, and how the new role could position you for future advancements.

Pursuing advanced education is another avenue that holds the potential to significantly impact your career trajectory and, consequently, your financial future. The decision to further your education should be aligned with clear career goals. Evaluate the return on investment by considering the cost of education, the time commitment, and the potential increase in earning power post-graduation. If you are thinking about going to or back to school, you also want to ask yourself whether you're going to be a full time student and part time worker, or part time student and full time worker. If you're already working, be sure to explore employer-sponsored education programs that might alleviate the financial burden while advancing your skills and marketability.

Embracing leadership roles, on the other hand, often comes with increased responsibilities and the potential for higher earnings. However, it also demands a greater time commitment, possibly impacting your work-life balance. Assessing your readiness for leadership, both personally and professionally, is crucial. Consider seeking mentorship to navigate the complexities of leadership and to aid in making informed decisions. Moreover, developing a robust network can provide insights and opportunities that might prove invaluable as you ascend into leadership positions.

Each of these pivotal moments requires a well-thought-out strategy and a deep understanding of your personal and financial long-term goals. They also demand a willingness to adapt and learn. By seeking advice from trusted mentors, continuously expanding your knowledge, and evaluating the potential risks and rewards, you'll be better positioned to make informed decisions that can positively shape your financial destiny. Moreover, it's crucial to maintain a holistic view. Your career decisions should not only align with your financial goals but also with your personal values, lifestyle preferences, and long-term life objectives. It's about creating a harmonious balance that propels you towards a fulfilling career and a robust financial future.

Through this guided exploration of career-defining decisions, you'll be empowered to navigate the complex landscape of career advancement with a clear vision and a strategic approach, thereby crafting a financial destiny that resonates with your ambitions and aspirations.

"I won't just break glass ceilings, I'll redesign the entire floor plan."

-Anonymous

Total Compensation

Your paycheck isn't the only thing that matters when you're evaluating a job offer. Employee benefits are an overlooked part in choosing your employer.

- **Health care -** Understanding your employee coverage levels, premiums, deductibles, and out-of-pocket costs associated with your health insurance can help you choose the right plan for your needs. Moreover, familiarizing yourself with Health Savings Accounts (HSAs) and Flexible Spending Accounts (FSAs) can provide additional avenues for saving and covering healthcare costs.

- **Retirement accounts-** Your employer may offer a 401(k) or a similar retirement savings plan. Contributing to these plans, especially if your employer provides a match, is a straightforward way to bolster your retirement savings. Understanding the contribution limits, employer matching details, and the investment options within your retirement account is crucial for optimizing this benefit.

- **Other perks-** Additionally, it's wise to explore other perks that may be available to you. These could range from tuition reimbursement programs, which can aid in furthering your education, to wellness programs that might offer discounts on gym memberships or other health-related services. Don't overlook potentially valuable benefits like life and disability insurance, employee assistance programs, and commuting or parking reimbursements. These benefits can have incredible value in that the reduce what you pay out of pocket for health or legal services, decrease your tax burden, or help you better weather a health emergency if you have if you become ill or injured.

Some employers offer stock options or employee stock purchase plans (ESPPs) as part of their benefits package. These programs allow you to buy company stock, often at a discounted rate, which could provide an additional avenue for financial growth. Learning the ropes of your benefits package isn't merely about understanding what's available to you; it's about strategically utilizing these benefits to enhance your financial situation. For instance, maximizing your 401(k) contributions, especially if there's an employer match, is akin to receiving free money towards your retirement. Similarly, selecting the right health insurance plan and contributing to an HSA or FSA can provide tax advantages and help offset healthcare costs.

Be sure to review and adjust your benefits selections every year and anytime you change jobs. Your needs may change over time, and ensuring your benefits align with your current circumstances is essential for getting the most value from them.

These resources, when harnessed correctly, can significantly bolster your financial stability. So, take the time to understand your benefits package—it's a pivotal step towards a more secure financial future.

Aligning Your Goals with Monetary Realities

Your career is not just about a job; it's about a journey that can significantly impact your financial future. To ensure that this journey aligns with your financial aspirations, it's crucial to start by aligning your career goals with monetary realities. Begin by acknowledging that your career decisions and financial goals are intricately interconnected. Where you work, what you do, and how you progress in your career can significantly affect your financial health. Therefore, it's essential to set career goals that complement your financial ambitions.

The first step in this alignment process is to **clearly define your career goals.** What are your professional aspirations? Do you want to climb the corporate ladder, start your own business, or pursue a creative career? Be specific about your goals. Once you have a clear vision, you can tailor your financial strategy accordingly.

Next, **take a deep dive into your financial aspirations**. What kind of lifestyle do you desire? Do you have specific financial milestones like buying a home, saving for retirement, or paying off debt on your list? Knowing your financial objectives will help you map out the financial resources you need to support your career goals. With your career and financial goals in mind, it's time to create a roadmap. This plan should outline the steps you need to take to achieve your professional and financial objectives.

Consider short-term and long-term milestones, and be realistic about the time and effort required to reach them. Regularly assess how well your career goals align with your monetary realities. Are you making progress towards your financial milestones while pursuing your dream career? If not, it may be time to make adjustments. Be open to modifying your goals or financial strategies to maintain alignment. Lastly, stay committed to the alignment process. It's easy to get caught up in the day-to-day demands of your career, but regularly reassessing and readjusting your goals and financial strategies will help you stay on track.

"I find that the most certain way to get what you want is to ask, directly and explicitly."

-Kara Goldin

Nurturing Connections that Boost Your Bottom Line

When you are starting a job search, you might think the first step is to update your resume. Wrong! You actually need to check your budget. If you don't deeply understand what it cost you to live, and whether you have any new or increased expenses coming up, you are almost guaranteed to leave money on the table.

Once you've checked and recalibrated your magic number, you can move on to evaluating potential employers. You'll want to get any information you can on growth opportunities, the company culture, and how a potential job change aligns with your long-term career objectives. Weighing the potential increase in salary, better benefits, and improved work-life balance against the risks and the unknowns is part of this pivotal decision- making process. It's also prudent to consider the stability and reputation of the prospective employer, and how the new role could position you for future advancements.

Pursuing advanced education is another avenue that holds the potential to significantly impact your career trajectory and, consequently, your financial future. The decision to further your education should be aligned with clear career goals. Evaluate the return on investment by considering the cost of education, the time commitment, and the potential increase in earning power post-graduation. If you are thinking about going to or back to school, you also want to ask yourself whether you're going to be a full time student and part time worker, or part time student and full time worker. If you're already working, be sure to explore employer-sponsored education programs that might alleviate the financial burden while advancing your skills and marketability.

The value of networking cannot be overstated. Networking isn't just about building a list of contacts; it's about nurturing relationships that can significantly impact your financial growth. In this section, we'll explore the role networking plays in your financial journey and provide you with actionable strategies to leverage the power of connections.

Before delving into networking strategies, it's essential to understand why networking matters for your financial growth. Networking can open doors to new opportunities, expose you to industry insights, and provide you with valuable mentors or advisors. These connections can lead to career advancements, salary increases, and even entrepreneurial ventures. Set clear and strategic networking goals aligned with your career and financial objectives. Do you aim to advance in your current field, explore a new industry, or find potential investors for your business? Defining your networking objectives will guide your efforts and help you focus on the right connections.

A well-rounded network includes professionals from various backgrounds and industries. Don't limit your network to only those who share your current career path. Diverse connections can offer fresh perspectives and unique opportunities that you might not find within your immediate circle, it also isn't about collecting business cards or LinkedIn connections. It's about building authentic relationships and Investing time in getting to know your connections on a personal level. Remember birthdays, inquire about their interests, and offer assistance when possible. These genuine connections can become valuable allies. Combine online and offline networking to maximize your reach and connections.

Understanding networking etiquette is essential. Always be respectful of people's time, follow up promptly after meetings or events, and offer help or support without expecting immediate returns. Building a reputation for reliability and professionalism can enhance your networking effectiveness. Regularly assess the impact of your networking efforts. Are you seeing tangible financial benefits, such as new job opportunities, increased income, or business growth? If not, revisit your networking strategy and adjust it as needed.

Strategic Planning

Active Listening - Pay close attention during conversations, ask thoughtful questions, and show genuine interest in others' experiences.

Give Before You Get - Offer assistance, share your knowledge, or provide referrals without expecting immediate returns.
If you need something, ask clearly and directly. Generally speaking people want to be helpful, having a clear "ask" makes it easy for them to know what help you're looking for.

Follow-Up - After initial meetings, promptly follow up with personalized messages or invitations for further discussions.

Leverage Mutual Connections - Mutual contacts can introduce you to valuable connections in their network.

Authentic relationships are more likely to lead to valuable collaborations, career advancements, and financial opportunities. Strategic networking involves identifying and connecting with professionals who can contribute to your career and financial objectives. These connections may encompass mentors, potential employers, business partners, or industry experts.

In a world filled with professionals, it's essential to stand out. Effective communication and the showcasing of your expertise are key components of creating a lasting positive impression.

Strategic relationships, whether in your professional or personal life, are not immune to challenges. Even the most carefully cultivated partnerships can encounter obstacles. These challenges often stem from various factors, such as differences in priorities, changing circumstances, or unexpected conflicts of interest. One common challenge in strategic relationships is conflicts of interest. These conflicts can arise when your goals or interests diverge from those of your partner. To address these conflicts effectively, it's essential to understanding the root cause of the conflict; Is it a clash of priorities, differences in long-term objectives, or a simple misunderstanding. Encourage transparent communication with your strategic partner. Express your concerns, listen actively to their perspective, and work together to find common ground. Instead of approaching conflicts as zero-sum games, aim for solutions where both parties benefit. This approach preserves the value of the relationship and fosters a sense of collaboration.

Circumstances change over time, and strategic relationships must adapt accordingly. Whether it's shifts in the market, alterations in business objectives, or personal life changes, being flexible is essential. To navigate these evolving circumstances Periodically review your objectives and those of your strategic partner. Are they still aligned, or have there been significant changes? Keep the lines of communication open to discuss any shifts in circumstances promptly. Transparency and flexibility are key to adapting effectively, and If significant changes make the original terms of your relationship obsolete, be willing to renegotiate. This demonstrates your commitment to a mutually beneficial partnership.

Trust as a Cornerstone

Trust is the foundation of any strategic relationship, and trust often relies on the protection of sensitive and confidential information. To safeguard privacy and confidentiality Establish clear guidelines, define what information is considered confidential and establish protocols for handling and sharing this data. Use secure communication channels and Ensure that any shared information is transmitted and stored securely, reducing the risk of unauthorized access. Always respect the boundaries and privacy preferences of your strategic partner. This builds trust and reinforces your professionalism.

The Elevator Pitch: Carving Impressions That Command Respect

Understanding the impact of first impressions is crucial. Research shows that people often form judgments about others within the first few seconds of meeting. Recognizing this fact underscores the importance of making these initial moments count. Authenticity is key when creating lasting first impressions. It means being true to yourself and not trying to be someone you're not. Confidence plays a pivotal role here. When you're genuinely confident in who you are, it radiates, making others more likely to trust and respect you.

Non-verbal cues often speak louder than words. A caveat that this is true in the US context, if you're an international reader, these tips may not apply. Let's delve into the nuances of body language starting with posture; Standing or sitting up straight exudes confidence and attentiveness, and Appropriate hand gestures can enhance your message, but excessive or inappropriate gestures can distract. Active listening is a critical component of effective verbal communication. techniques for being fully present during conversations can include asking open-ended questions, encouraging others to share more, and fostering meaningful discussions.

A positive mindset is contagious and can be instrumental in leaving a favorable impression. strategies for cultivating optimism include Using positive affirmations to reshape your thinking, Practicing mindfulness to stay present and grounded and Visualizing successful interactions and outcomes. Remember, creating connections during initial interactions is about more than just making a good impression. It's about building authentic relationships that can lead to valuable opportunities and professional growth. By understanding and avoiding common pitfalls, such as appearing disinterested or using negative language, you can enhance your networking skills and forge lasting connections in your career journey.

Networking is a dynamic process that evolves over time, and with practice, you'll become more adept at navigating its intricacies. Embrace opportunities to meet new people, learn from their experiences, and offer your insights in return. By approaching networking with intention, developing meaningful connections, and applying the strategies we discussed you're not only setting the stage for career success but also aligning your professional efforts with your financial aspirations.

Quest for Fiscal Finesse: Seeking Roles that Align with Financial Objectives

Before making any career choices, it's crucial to revisit what we discussed in the "Real Money Talk" chapter. What does it cost you to live? What's your magic number, your baseline? This understanding is the foundation upon which you'll build your career and financial future. Your job choices should align with your financial goals. It is essential to have a clear understanding of your financial situation.

Create a concise yet impactful elevator pitch that introduces yourself, highlights your strengths, and communicates your career aspirations. Tailor your pitch to resonate with different audiences, whether you're speaking with industry professionals or potential employers. Thoroughly investigate the company's history, culture, and values through online resources, company websites, and news articles. Identify key individuals within the organization, such as executives or department heads, and learn about their roles. Use your research to align your responses with the company's mission and values during interviews.

The STAR Technique

Understand the STAR (Situation,Task, Action, Result) technique and its application in structuring responses to behavioral interview questions. Practice using the STAR method to showcase your qualifications and problem-solving skills effectively. Develop a repository of specific examples from your past experiences to draw from during interviews.

Salary Negotiation Mastery: Securing Your Financial Future

Break down your compensation package into its components, including base salary, bonuses, stock options, retirement benefits, and healthcare coverage. Analyze how each element contributes to your overall compensation and financial stability. Research industry standards and salary benchmarks to ensure you're receiving fair compensation then Assess your unique value proposition by considering your skills, experience, and the demand for your expertise in the job market. Set clear negotiation objectives based on your financial goals and career aspirations. Develop a strategy that includes a range for your desired salary, allowing room for negotiation.

Anticipate common objections and challenges that may arise during salary negotiations, such as concerns about budget constraints or competing job offers. Prepare persuasive responses and counterarguments to address these challenges effectively. Maintain professionalism and composure throughout the negotiation process, even when faced with resistance. As you move forward in your career journey, remember that your professional path and financial future are intertwined. Each career decision you make has the potential to impact your financial well-being positively or negatively.

"Always stay gracious, best revenge is your paper."
-*Beyoncé*

Income Tracker

Start Date: ______________________ End Date: ______________________

	DATE	INCOME	TYPE	AMOUNT
1				
2				
3				
4				
5				
6				
7				
8				
9				
10				
11				
12				
13				
14				
15				

Notes

My Career Map

Fill in the tiles to document your career highlights and map your earnings. To get your annualized salary amount, multiply your hourly rate by 2,080 for full time work.

First job	Most recent job	Dream job
Title:	Title:	Employer:
Pay:	Pay:	Title:
I loved:	I love:	Pay:
I didn't love:	I would change:	Why this excites me:

Best/ Favorite job	Most impressive title	Worst job
Title:	Title:	Title:
Pay:	Pay:	Pay:
I loved:	I loved:	I loved:
I didn't love:	I didn't love:	I didn't love:

Map your salary history here

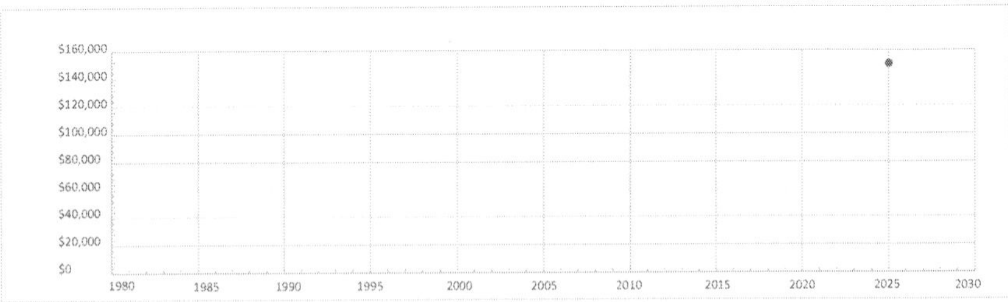

Chapter Nine

Look At You Adulting

As you step into the realm of adulthood, a new chapter of life unfolds—one that's rich with opportunities, challenges, and the promise of financial independence. This chapter is your compass to navigate the uncharted waters of grown-up finances.

Alexa's graduation day marked not just the end of her academic years but also the beginning of a more formidable venture into adulthood. As the reality of pending bills and financial responsibilities began to set in, she knew it was time to confront them head-on. Her first order of business was to figure out her monthly expenses. Rent, utilities, and groceries were tallied alongside her impending student loan payments. With a clear-eyed view of her outflows, Alexa crafted a meticulous budget to keep her spending in check. With her budget in place, Alexa's focus shifted to her income. Job hunting became her full-time occupation post-graduation. She revamped her resume, practiced interview techniques, and networked relentlessly within her chosen field.

Her dedication bore fruit when she accepted a position that not only offered her a stable income but also pointed her toward a promising career path. Student loans, however, were the specter that haunted her newfound financial landscape. Alexa approached them with a strategy to balance aggressive repayment without stretching her budget too thin. She became disciplined about her repayments, intent on freeing herself from the debt as expediently as possible.

Parallel to managing her debts, Alexa understood the importance of savings. She started small, consistently funneling a portion of her income into an emergency fund. This safety net grew, providing her with a buffer against life's unpredictabilities. With the basics of budgeting, debt management, and savings underway, Alexa looked to the horizon —her future. She educated herself on investment vehicles, retirement accounts, and the benefits of early and consistent investment. Contributions to her 401(k) began, and she opened an IRA, nurturing the seeds of her long-term financial security.

Years of diligence and smart financial habits steered Alexa to where she is today. Debt became a thing of the past, investments matured, and the notion of financial independence transformed from a distant goal to her living reality.

"Knock me down nine times but
I get up ten"

-Cardi B

Gaining Financial independence

Navigating your post-grad paycheck is a rite of passage into financial adulthood, marking the beginning of your journey toward financial independence. Managing your income effectively is the cornerstone of this new chapter.

Upon receiving that first paycheck, it's crucial to start with a plan. Begin by identifying your fixed expenses such as housing, utilities, student loans, and any other regular payments. These are your financial anchors, and they must be covered first and foremost. *Next*, prioritize the creation of an emergency fund. Decide on a percentage of your paycheck that can be directed into savings. Even if it's a small amount at first, this fund is your financial safety net, designed to protect you from unforeseen expenses. With your necessities and emergency fund in place, consider your discretionary spending. This is the portion of your income that can be allocated towards wants rather than needs. Be strategic about this spending to ensure that you can enjoy the present while still planning for the future.

Investing is the next step in securing your financial independence. Investigate options like employer-sponsored retirement plans, especially if they offer matching contributions. If such a plan isn't available, look into opening an Individual Retirement Account (IRA). Remember, the earlier you start investing, the more you benefit from compound interest over time.Lastly, remain adaptable. As you progress in your career and your financial situation evolves, revisit and revise your budget.

Salary increases, unexpected bills, or new financial goals will require adjustments to your financial plan.

Paycheck Playbook: Setting the Foundation for Fiscal Stability

The "Paycheck Playbook" is your guide to fiscal stability from the very first day you start earning. Here's how to approach it, ***in this order***

1. **Build an Oh! Sh*t Fund**: Before anything else, accumulate $1,000 in a savings account. This is your immediate buffer against life's unexpected moments. It's not meant to cover all emergencies, but it will provide you with critical breathing room.
2. **Make and Work Your Debt Plan**: Tackle your debts with a strategic plan. List them out, determine which to pay off first (typically those with the highest interest), and set up a payment schedule. This might involve consolidating debts or negotiating payment terms.
3. **Contribute to Retirement**: If your employer offers a retirement plan, like a 401(k), start contributing enough to get the full company match. It's essentially free money that you don't want to miss out on.
4. **Max Contribution to a Roth IRA**: Once you're getting the full match from your employer's retirement plan, aim to max out contributions to a Roth IRA, if you qualify. The benefit of a Roth IRA is that your money grows tax-free, and you can withdraw it tax-free in retirement.
5. **Build up Savings to 3-6 Months of Expenses**: Return to your savings account and work toward having 3-6 months' worth of living expenses saved. This is a robust emergency fund that can carry you through more significant financial obstacles like job loss or major medical bills.
6. **Max Out 401(k)/403(b) Contributions**: With a solid emergency fund in place, you can focus on maximizing your 401(k) or 403(b) contributions. The more you save now, the more you'll have in retirement thanks to compound interest.
7. **Fund Children's Education (If Applicable)**: If you have children and plan to contribute to their education, now is the time to explore education savings accounts like 529 plans. Like retirement savings, the sooner you start,

the better, but after you have the other items in the list in a good place.

I recommend tackling your finances in this order so that you can establish the habit of prioritizing your own financial standing and maximize tax advantages. Both Roth IRAs and 401(k)s offer liquidity through the possibility of borrowing against them if dire circumstances arise, allowing you to pay interest back into your own accounts instead of to a lender. Prioritizing your retirement savings early on feeds the 'compound interest beast,' allowing your wealth to grow substantially over time. It's critical to capitalize on this as early as possible for your own financial health.

Children's education savings are positioned later in the sequence. This is because, typically, your earning power will increase as your career progresses, which should give you greater capacity to support your children's educational expenses when the time comes. It's a strategic move to ensure you're not sacrificing your own financial security for future costs.

Mastering your fiscal responsibilities becomes not just a chapter in a book, but chapters in your life. Adulthood is peppered with both freedoms and obligations, the most immediate of which is the financial responsibility that comes with living on your own.

Lease - Utilities - Insurance

A lease is not just a document, but a commitment that frames your financial routine. Take the time to understand each provision and Know your obligations. What are you responsible for beyond the rent? Anticipate and budget for potential rent hikes at lease renewal. Clarify the terms for breaking the lease because let's face it, life is unpredictable. It's essential to know the financial implications if you need to move out early.

Next in line are the utilities — **electricity, water, gas, and internet.** These are not just bills; they represent the comforts and necessities of modern life. Conduct an energy audit and Identify where you can make cost-saving adjustments, like insulating windows or upgrading to energy-efficient appliances. Some utility companies offer plans that average your yearly consumption into equal monthly payments to avoid seasonal spikes.

Navigating insurance is an exercise in balancing cost against risk. If you have an emergency fund, consider increasing your deductibles to lower your premiums, and purchasing multiple policies from the same provider can often lead to discounts. By mastering these financial responsibilities, you equip yourself with a toolkit for navigating the complexities of economic life.

“In the grand scheme of things, it’s not about what you take, darling, but what you leave behind.”

-Anonymous

Bills on Bills: Taming Monthly Expenses With Organized Precision

When it comes to managing bills, the key to tranquility and financial order is the development of a personalized system. For some, this might mean setting up calendar reminders a week in advance of each due date, ensuring there's ample time to review the charges and address any discrepancies before making a payment. For the technologically inclined, automating payments might be the method of choice, with arrangements made for money to be debited directly from a checking account or charged to a credit card, thus guaranteeing that payments are never missed.

Imagine this, it's the first of the month, and instead of feeling a sense of dread, there's calm. Whichever system you choose, the outcome is a streamlined process that works seamlessly within the fabric of your life. Bills are paid on time, every time, without the panic or the hassle of last- minute payments. It's a strategy not just for financial health, but for peace of mind.

In refining your bill-paying system, it's crucial to consider the fluid nature of life and finances. As such, building a system that's not only effective but also adaptable is essential. However, the system you choose should not be rigid. Life changes, such as a fluctuating income or an unexpected expense, necessitate flexibility in how you manage your bills. As your financial situation evolves, so too might your bill-paying strategy. You may find that you need to build in a buffer within your account, or perhaps, start using financial tools that offer predictive features to help you anticipate monthly cash flow. Consistently reviewing and adjusting your approach is key. For instance, if your expenses increase, you may need to monitor your spending more closely to stay within your budget. Employing budgeting apps or financial management software can offer real- time insights and alerts to keep you on track.

Balancing Income and Expenditures

Balancing income and expenditure is a continuous journey that ensures your finances stay afloat. Here's how you can apply this principle in your life.

First, take a moment to understand the nature of your income. Is it steady and predictable, or does it ebb and flow? Knowing this helps determine the flexibility of your financial plan. *Then*, examine your expenditures with the eye of an accountant. Divide them into clear categories, This gives you a blueprint of where your money goes each month. With your income and expenses laid out, it's time to draft your master plan.

Regular check-ins on your budget are crucial and It ensures you stay on course, making adjustments as needed, whether that's cutting back on discretionary spending or finding ways to boost your income. Lastly, Are there milestones you wish to reach? Whether it's retiring comfortably, owning a home, or funding an education, direct any financial surplus towards these long-term goals.

Guiding Your Legacy: Setting the Stage for Lifelong Financial Security

When considering life insurance, the process should begin with a clear assessment of why you need it. The primary purpose of life insurance is to provide financial support to the people who depend on your income if you were to pass away unexpectedly. To determine the appropriate amount of life insurance, several key factors must be taken into account.

One of the main functions of life insurance is to replace your income for those who depend on it. A common approach is to aim for a policy payout that is 10 to 12 times your annual income. This can provide a financial buffer that allows your family to maintain their standard of living.

Your life insurance should cover your outstanding debts, including mortgage, car loans, credit card debt, and any other liabilities. This ensures that your family won't be burdened by debt during an already difficult time. Consider future financial obligations such as college tuition for children or retirement funds for your spouse. Factoring in these expenses can help you decide on the amount of coverage needed. Life insurance can also cover funeral costs, estate settlement fees, and any medical bills that may not be covered by health insurance.

In the simplest terms, ask yourself, how much time do you want your loved ones to have before they have to make changes to their lifestyle when they no longer have your income? Being able to minimize changes to their home, school, and standard of living can help the grieving process because they don't have the added financial stress on top of the toll of grief. If you're just starting out, here's an easy way to work yourself up this "ladder" as your finances get better.

1. *Final expense insurance* - this is insurance that covers the expenses your loved ones will pay to cover the final expenses and your memorial. If you don't have much room in your budget, this helps prevent your family from having to go into debt or use crowd funding to say their goodbyes to your physical body

2. *20,000* - depending on the size of your family and current expenses, $20,000 in a term life insurance policy on top of a final expense policy will help ease the initial shock of your loss for at least a short amount of time

3. *2x your annual salary* - a policy that is 2x your salary will buy your family 1.5 - 2 years of time before they have to make major changes like selling a house or car due to finances.

4. *5x your annual salary* - same as above, but with a longer run way

5. ***10-15x your annual salary*** - this might allow your children to become adults or at least teenagers with the benefit of your financial resources

Policy Type

Decide between term life insurance, which covers you for a specified period (usually 10-30 years), and is less expensive, or permanent life insurance, like whole life, which lasts your entire lifetime and includes an investment component.
Your own financial situation and age will influence the type and amount of coverage you need. Once you've calculated the total financial support your dependents would require, you can then compare life insurance policies. It's advisable to get quotes from multiple providers to find the best rate for the coverage you need. Remember, the goal of life insurance is to provide peace of mind, knowing that your loved ones will be financially protected in your absence.

Continuous Personal Growth: Embracing Learning Beyond The Classroom

As you transition from the structure of classroom learning, the real challenge begins; to keep learning in a world without syllabi and due dates. To thrive in this environment, adopt a self-driven approach to expand your financial knowledge. You can start by setting up a personal curriculum that addresses gaps in your understanding. Whether it's the basics of budgeting or the complexities of investment portfolios, identify the areas you want to strengthen. Make a habit of staying informed. Regularly reading financial news or subscribing to finance-related newsletters can keep you updated on market trends and economic shifts. This habit will help you make informed decisions about your own finances.

Don't be shy to engage in financial communities online or in person, Participating in forums, or joining investment clubs can provide a support system and a knowledge network that classroom learning cannot. Consider the value of mentorship. Reach out to professionals in the field you're interested in, and don't hesitate to ask for advice or insight. A mentor can offer guidance based on real-world experience, which is invaluable for personal and professional growth. Remember, the objective is to integrate continuous learning into your lifestyle. You might listen to a finance podcast on your commute, read an investing book before bed, or research real estate during lunch breaks. This seamless integration ensures that learning becomes a natural part of your daily routine.

Personal development should extend beyond financial knowledge. Enhancing your soft skills, like communication and critical thinking, can have a direct impact on your financial success. Negotiation skills, for example, can help you secure better salaries or investment deals. By embracing learning as a lifelong endeavor, you're not just preparing for financial independence; you're ensuring it. The world beyond the classroom is rich with lessons waiting to be discovered, and your proactive approach to learning is the key to unlocking them.

This marks the commencement of your financial journey as a self-reliant adult. navigate bills, investments, and savings with confidence, and create a future that radiates financial well-being and enduring success.

"What do you want? What do you want your life to be? What do you want your testimony to be?"

-Viola Davis

Income & Expense Tracker

Use this activity sheet to record and manage your monthly financial flows.

month	income	expenses	difference	notes
JANUARY				
FEBRUARY				
MARCH				
APRIL				
MAY				
JUNE				
JULY				
AUGUST				
SEPTEMBER				
OCTOBER				
NOVEMBER				
DECEMBER				
TOTAL				

WHAT WERE THE BEST MONTHS? WHY?

WHAT WERE THE WORST MONTHS? WHY?

Chapter Ten
And One Last Thing...

Look back at it

As we reach the final chapter of this empowering journey, it's time to look back and reflect on the remarkable transformation you've undergone. This summary serves as both a review and a celebration of the growth, insights, and financial knowledge you've gained along the way. We've covered an incredible amount of ground. You've acquired knowledge, insights, and skills that will transform your financial perspective and, ultimately, your life. Let's take a moment to glance back at some of the most valuable lessons and key insights that have shaped your financial journey.

Think back to the early chapters, where you took the brave step of unmasking your spending habits and examining your financial values. You learned that every purchase you make is a statement, and you've since made those statements align with your financial goals. Take a moment to review the budget you created and how it has evolved. Are you now allocating your resources more effectively and in alignment with your financial goals?

You've delved into the world of stocks, bonds, and beyond, and not only decoded the mechanics of investing but also grasped how it can be aligned with your finances. When we spoke about savings and debt, you discovered the importance of building a financial safety net and the impact it had on your financial health. Armed with this knowledge, you've taken steps to secure your financial future. Take a moment to assess your debt situation. Have you made progress in reducing harmful debt while leveraging good debt for financial growth?

Your career plays a significant role in your financial journey. Reflect on the career decisions you've made and how they align with your financial objectives. Do you have new career aspirations? Are you on a path that supports your long- term financial? This goes hand in hand with your professional relationships and new networking skills. By this point, you understand the power of connections in the world of careers and finances, and can build meaningful relationships and harness them to uncover hidden opportunities.

Carrying Forward Wisdom

Integrating Key Principles Into Your Future

Now, as you stand at the cusp of concluding this journey, remember that your financial education never stops. Continue seeking opportunities to enhance your financial knowledge, staying attuned to industry changes and evolving trends. Just as you've adapted your strategies throughout this journey, be open to adjusting your financial plans as your life evolves.

As your money mentor, I want to acknowledge your unwavering commitment to improving your financial well-being. Celebrate every achievement, no matter how big or small, and keep setting meaningful financial goals that resonate with your values and aspirations.

Remember the power of consistency and discipline in your financial habits, and I want to emphasize that your financial future is bright. Your journey doesn't end here; it's an ongoing path to prosperity. Every financial decision you make contributes to your long-term success.

You've embraced financial wisdom, laughed in the face of financial challenges, and paved your way to financial empowerment. As you step into your future, carry the lessons, the humor, and the resilience that you've found within these pages. Cheers to a life rich in both financial understanding and fulfilled dreams... Until we meet again in another book.

"You can rest, and everything that's gonna happen for you is still gonna happen for you"

-Keke Palmer

Fiscal Dreams

Write out your aspirations for a financially empowered future

If you're looking for more, check out the *FinanSis* podcast wherever you get podcasts. Visit **darlabishop.com/worksheets** for bonus content and to download the activity sheets that appear throughout the book.

Here is my top 10 favorite personal finance and self-help books:

- *We Should All Be Millionaires by Rachel rodgers*
- *The Millionaire next door by Thomas Stanley*
- *Total Money Makeover by Dave Ramsey*
- *Soul of Money by Lynne Twist*
- *The Index Card: Why Personal Finance Doesn't have to be Complicated by Helaine Olen and Harold Pollack*
- *Secrets of Six Figure Women by Barbara Stanny*
- *The Secret by Rhonda Byrne*
- *Ask For More: 10 Questions to Negotiate Anything by Alexandra Carter*
- *Sis, You're Copper: An Alchemy to Shine by Jess Jackson*
- *Rich Dad Advisors, Tax Free Wealth by Tom Wheelwritght*

"Just believe in yourself. Even if you don't, pretend that you do and at some point you will"

-Venus Williams

Appedix: Activity Sheets

Hmm.. do you really need it?

This worksheet provides an objective perspective on your potential purchases, helping to ensure that it's a wise and beneficial decision.

Do I need this item or do I just want it?

Will this purchase fulfill a basic necessity or is it for pleasure?

____

____

____

Do I need this item How often will I use this item?

Is it a one-time use or will it be used regularly?

____

____

____

Is the cost of the item justified by the value it provides?

Am I paying for quality or just for the brand?

____

____

____

Does this purchase fit within my current budget?

Will buying this now cause financial strain in the near future?

____

____

____

Is this a long-term investment or a short-term gratification?

Will this item hold its value over time?

____

____

____

Am I making this purchase on impulse or after careful consideration?

Am I buying this to feel better emotionally?

____

____

____

The Spending Spectrum

Rank your shopping desires by writing them in the segment that best corresponds with their importance.

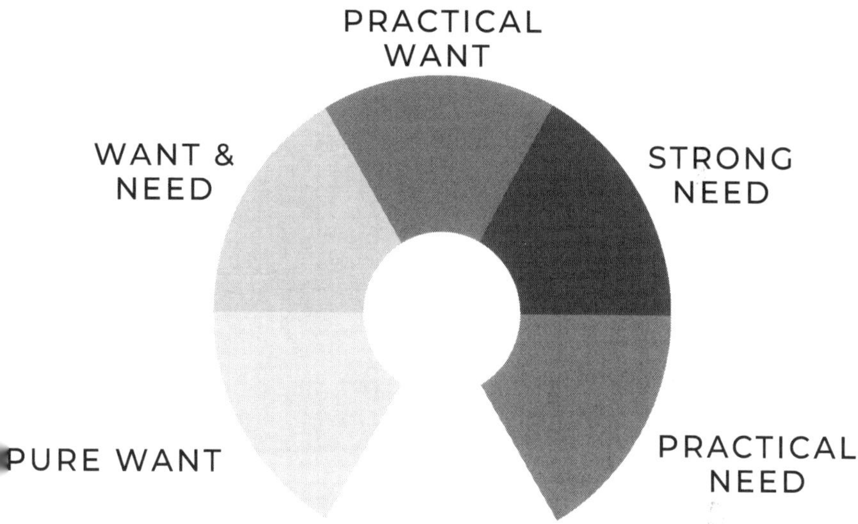

Progress Tracker

Write a goal in each spot. Color each spot in when you reach the corresponding milestone.

Use this worksheet to map out your budget.

Monthly Budget

MONTH

VARIABLE / OTHER EXPENSES			
Date	Description	Notes	Amount

SAVINGS				
Account	Name	Starting Balance	Amount	End Balance

TOTALS	
Total Income	
Minus fixed expenses	
Minus savings	
Left for variable expenses	
End Balance	

The Ultimate Finance Tracker

Education

DATE	AMOUNT

Travel

DATE	AMOUNT

Gifts

DATE	AMOUNT

Personal Spending

DATE	AMOUNT

Payment Progress Tracker

Use this activity sheet to Document your progress towards debt liberation

CREDITOR

ACCOUNT NO

START BALANCE

CREDIT LIMIT

TARGET PAYOFF DATE

TYPE

MINIMUM PAYMENT

INTEREST RATE

BALANCE	MINIMUM PAYMENT	AMOUNT PAID	DATE PAID	CONFIRMATION

NOTES:

Think of a goal that youve been trying to reach.
Everytime to reach a saving Milestone, fill in the tracker.

Dream Savings Tracker

100% ....

90% ....

80% ....

70% ....

60% ....

50% ....

40% ....

30% ....

20% ....

10% ....

Start: ....

I'm saving for

Why I'm saving for this

Amount

Deadline

Yearly Saving Goals

Use this calendar to map out your yearly savings goals.

JANUARY	FEBRUARY	MARCH
APRIL	MAY	JUNE
JULY	AUGUST	SEPTEMBER
OCOTBER	NOVEMBER	DECEMBER

The Deduction Circle

Use the list on the previous page to help you identify potential deductions and credits. Fill in each slice on this page if you qualify for any of the deductions or credits mentioned.

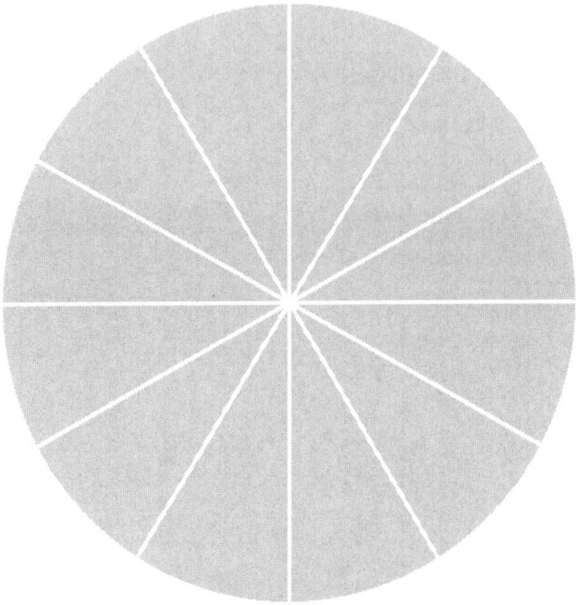

NOTES

Investment Dreamboard

Jot down your investment goals using this investment dreamboard. Color in the first column once you've invested in the corresponding company.

INVESTED?	TYPE/NAME	COST	AMOUNT	DATE
		TOTAL		

Donation Tracker

Use this activity sheet to track your donations for the month. Put an "X" through each day you donated or participated in anything philanthropic

1	2	3	4	5	6	7	8
9	10	11	12	13	14	15	16
17	18	19	20	21	22	23	24
25	26	27	28	29	30	31	

NOTES

Income Tracker

Start Date: ____________________ End Date: ____________________

	DATE	INCOME	TYPE	AMOUNT
1				
2				
3				
4				
5				
6				
7				
8				
9				
10				
11				
12				
13				
14				
15				

Notes

My Career Map

Fill in the tiles to document your career highlights and map your earnings. To get your annualized salary amount, multiply your hourly rate by 2,080 for full time work.

First job

Title:

Pay:

I loved:

I didn't love:

Most recent job

Title:

Pay:

I love:

I would change:

Dream job

Employer:

Title:

Pay:

Why this excites me:

Best/ Favorite job

Title:

Pay:

I loved:

I didn't love:

Most impressive title

Title:

Pay:

I loved:

I didn't love:

Worst job

Title:

Pay:

I loved:

I didn't love:

Map your salary history here

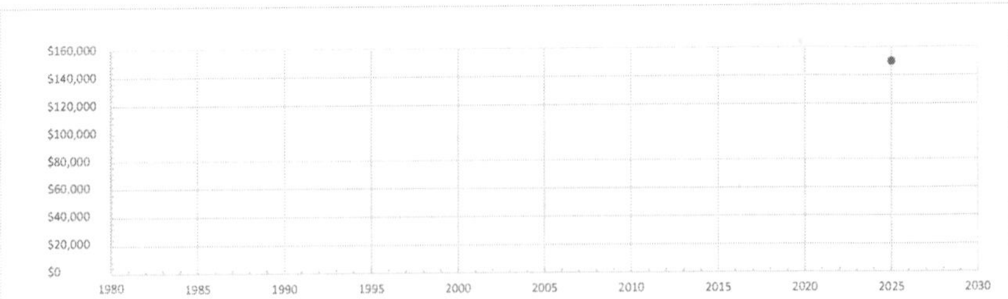

Income & Expense Tracker

Use this activity sheet to record and manage your monthly financial flows.

month	income	expenses	difference	notes
JANUARY				
FEBRUARY				
MARCH				
APRIL				
MAY				
JUNE				
JULY				
AUGUST				
SEPTEMBER				
OCTOBER				
NOVEMBER				
DECEMBER				
TOTAL				

WHAT WERE THE BEST MONTHS? WHY?

WHAT WERE THE WORST MONTHS? WHY?

Fiscal Dreams

Write out your aspirations for a financially empowered future.

Printed in Great Britain
by Amazon

54507342R00099